THE new rebellion*

HANDBOOK

*a holy uprising making real the extraordinary in everyday life

D1005501

The promise of being transformed and ignited to holy passion by understanding and beholding God's glorious personality is for all believers. No matter how weak or strong we feel, regardless of our previous failures, irrespective of our natural temperaments or personalities, each of us can be ablaze with passion for Jesus.

Mike Bickle

THE
new
rebellion*
HANDBOOK

*a holy uprising making real the
extraordinary in everyday life*

NELSON BOOKS
A Division of Thomas Nelson Publishers
Since 1798

www.thomasnelson.com

Copyright © 2006 by GRQ, Inc.
Brentwood, Tennessee

New Rebellion and its encircled cross logo are registered trademarks of GRQ, Inc.

All rights reserved. No portion of this book may be reproduced, stored in a retrieval system, or transmitted in any form or by any means—electronic, mechanical, photocopy, recording, scanning, or other—except for brief quotations in critical reviews or articles, without the prior written permission of the publisher.

Published in Nashville, Tennessee, by Thomas Nelson, Inc.

Nelson Books titles may be purchased in bulk for educational, business, fund-raising, or sales promotional use. For information, please e-mail SpecialMarkets@ThomasNelson.com.

Scripture quotations noted NKJV are from The New King James Version®. Copyright © 1979, 1980, 1982 by Thomas Nelson, Inc. Used by permission. All rights reserved. • Scripture quotations noted NCV are from The Holy Bible, New Century Version, copyright © 1987, 1988, 1991 by Word Publishing, a division of Thomas Nelson, Inc. All rights reserved. Used by permission. • Scripture quotations noted MSG are from The Message. Copyright © by Eugene H. Peterson 1993, 1994, 1995. Used by permission of NavPress Publishing Group. • Scripture quotations noted NIV are from the Holy Bible: New International Version®. Copyright © 1973, 1978, 1984 by International Bible Society. Used by permission of Zondervan Publishing House. All rights reserved. • Scripture quotations noted NLT are from the Holy Bible, New Living Translation, copyright © 1996. Used by permission of Tyndale House Publishers, Inc., Wheaton, Illinois 60189. All rights reserved. • Scripture quotations noted NASB are from the New American Standard Bible®, copyright © 1960, 1962, 1963, 1968, 1971, 1973, 1975, 1977, 1995 by The Lockman Foundation. Used by permission. • Scripture quotations noted HCSB have been taken from the Holman Christian Standard Bible®, Copyright © 1999, 2000, 2002, 2003 by Holman Bible Publishers. Used by permission. Holman Christian Standard Bible®, Holman CSB® and HCSB® are federally registered trademarks of Holman Bible Publishers.

Managing Editor: Lila Empson
Associate Editor: Bryan Norman
Manuscript: Jerome Daley
Design: Whisner Design Group, Tulsa, Oklahoma

ISBN 0-7852-1867-X

Printed in the United States of America

06 07 08 09 10 5 4 3 2 1

It's quite simple: Do what is fair and just to your neighbor, be compassionate and loyal in your love, and don't take yourself too seriously—take God seriously.

Micah 6:8 MSG

Contents

Introduction

The New Rebellion. What's it all about?

Rebellion occurs when oppression reaches a level that we can no longer tolerate in good conscience. It occurs when our vision for extraordinary living is more compelling than our urge for comfort. Oppression can be subtle. Sometimes we feel it inside our souls, and sometimes we feel it on the outside. Today's world is full of both kinds. Materialism numbs us from the outside while distraction and apathy work on us from the inside. When that happens, it's time to rebel.

The New Rebellion calls to today's emerging generation, to *your* generation. It calls to people who are disillusioned with MTV culture, tired of halfhearted Christianity. The New Rebellion calls to all of us who want to rise above the accepted norms of society and lay hold of a life beyond our wildest dreams. If that describes you, then join the uprising of ordinary men and women who have been captivated by an extraordinary call to holiness on planet Earth.

The New Rebellion series is designed to equip us with powerful tools for partnering with God to change the world. That means a dichotomy of choices for the man or woman who wants to be a Christ-follower: Engaged or non-engaged. Effective or non-effective. Rebel with a cause or well-intentioned bystander in the spiritual struggle for a generation.

The New Rebellion movement is for those of us who are intensely passionate for Jesus and are determined to live a purposeful life. This pure passion is in stark contrast with the unholy passions of the earth. Those of us who embrace the Rebellion have a fire in our eyes—a fire of love and triumph. We have a nothing-is-impossible mind-set. Jesus is not meek and mild to us; He is mighty and wild!

The New Rebellion generation is defined not by age or demographic. It includes the spiritually hungry of every age, culture, and gender who share a common passion to reach beyond a small life. It's time for courage and compassion to awaken a generation to its heavenly destiny. It's time for us to be who we're meant to be.

If this is for you and you're ready to change your world, *The New Rebellion Handbook* is a wealth of resources for your quest. Twenty-four real-world, cutting-edge themes of life are addressed here. Each one will challenge you with fresh ideas, biblical insights, and life applications. A wide array of music, books, and Web sites reinforce and fuel your mission. Stories of ancient and contemporary figures—rebels themselves—offer a compelling invitation into Kingdom purpose through Wisdom from the Past, and Wisdom from the Now. The Question, Top-Ten lists . . . there's a lot here to empower your life.

Dare to join the New Rebellion!

This army is unique. When this army comes, it's large and mighty. It's so mighty that there has never been anything like it before. What's going to happen now will transcend what Paul did, what David did, and what Moses did.

Jack Deere

The Top Ten Reasons to Join the New Rebellion

10 You are intensely passionate for Jesus and His Kingdom!

9 You really want to live a life of eternal significance.

8 You resent the apathy that derails many of Jesus' followers.

7 You're willing to swim against today's social currents.

6 You know God is already stirring your heart for action.

5 You're looking for tools to empower your purpose.

4 You want to live out God's ancient wisdom in a relevant way.

3 You desire to experience God and invite others into that experience.

2 You're absolutely dedicated to Christ's lordship in your life.

1 You're ready to move in the power and authority of God.

A man can no more diminish
God's glory by refusing to worship
Him than a lunatic can put out the
sun by scribbling "darkness" on the
wall of his cell.

C. S. Lewis

Let's Get Vertical

The essence of worship is an unrestrained giving of yourself to your heart's greatest treasure. One thing, above all others, will lay hold of your deepest affection and truest allegiance. As a Christ-follower, your passion for Him will find genuine pleasure in giving—giving adoration, giving thanks, giving time and service, and giving attention throughout each day of your life. This is the beginning of worship.

Because worship connects you to the object of your highest devotion, it establishes a vital relationship, the most vital of all, in fact. It is a relationship destined for intimacy, as fantastic as that may sound. The greater the giving of yourself, the more freely your heart pours out delight and the deeper the intimacy between you and God. This is real Kingdom living. This is what you are made for.

Worship

the buzz

The object of your worship and the intensity of your worship will define your life. It has always been this way. So what's new about that? What's new is this generation. God has a unique purpose for every generation, and some generations accomplish their purpose better than others. But you have only one shot at it—one life to devote to this eternal mission of worship.

The New Rebellion generation seems to have made a more significant shift than usual from the prior one, and that's not without purpose. God is instigating a large-scale invasion of planet Earth, and His warriors are worshipers.

"From the days of John the Baptist until now," Jesus said, "the kingdom of heaven has been forcefully advancing, and forceful men lay hold of it." Matthew 11:12 NIV

"From the days of John the Baptist until now," Jesus said, "the kingdom of heaven has been forcefully advancing, and forceful men lay hold of it" (Matthew 11:12 NIV). There is a Holy Spirit–infused violence that is required to break free from the idols of this world and forge a new direction, a Kingdom direction.

So if the purpose of a new generation of worshipers is to advance the Kingdom of God, what exactly is this Kingdom? Good question. The Kingdom is the realm ruled by the King—it is a spiritual world that overlaps the natural world and seeks to establish the redemptive purposes and culture of heaven upon earth. As a citizen of God's

Kingdom, you are His agent to live out the values and intentions of God's realm within this natural realm. You can do this powerfully as a worshiper.

God's new generation of worshipers does not war against people or political parties or abortion clinics. You war, as Ephesians 6:12 declares, "against the evil rulers and authorities of the unseen world, against those mighty powers of darkness who rule this world, and against wicked spirits in the heavenly realms" (NLT).

Your inner worship of Jesus will transform your outer life as well. A heart set upon God's Kingdom will bring your life into stark contrast with the false gods worshiped by this world—money and power, sports and entertainment, youth and beauty. These are the idols that the New Rebellion scoffs at. They cannot compare with the splendor of God.

The things that contemporary culture worships are "takers"—that is, they demand your time and attention, your loyalty, and ultimately your very heart. In contrast, the object of your worship is the most generous Giver. The worship that you bring to Him

Your inner worship of Jesus will transform your outer life as well. A heart set upon God's Kingdom will bring your life into stark contrast with the false gods worshiped by this world—money and power, sports and entertainment, youth and beauty.

will find expression in a lavish, unrestrained giving of all you are and all you have. You are the new-generation worshiper. You are the New Rebellion.

Worship

the insight

There is a story of worship involving King David that you may not have noticed before. See what you think.

David was hunkered down in the cave of Adullam (see 2 Samuel 23). Foreign enemies were pressing him on one side, and his own mad, murderous king was pressing him on the other. David let out something between a sigh and a moan: *What I would give for a drink from Bethlehem's well right now!* Not much to ask for when your life is on the line, except for the slight fact that Bethlehem was in occupied territory.

> There is something about vulnerability, risk, and generosity that is intrinsic to the very core of worship.

A smile flickered across the lips of Shammah, one of David's warriors, and he discreetly caught the eye of Eleazar. Together with Josheb, they slipped out of the cave and began the thirty-mile round-trip through enemy country just to bring back a skin of water from one particular well.

Can you believe it? Those three risked everything merely to bring pleasure to the heart of their lord. Then, not content to thank them and drink, David recognized that this was a holy thing—too holy for him, in fact—and he poured the precious gift out as an offering to his Lord.

Did you catch it? That was worship in action. Worship is about recognizing worth. *Worth*-ship, if you will. David's band of brothers saw that their leader was worthy of their lives. David recognized the worth of their sacrifice and knew it belonged to Another.

There is something about vulnerability, risk, and generosity that is intrinsic to the very core of worship. You, too, will have numerous opportunities to recognize the worth of Kingdom character and Kingdom action. You will sense a divine invitation to risk for the sake of your Lord. Warring worshipers will swallow hard, pick up their spiritual weapons, and give themselves fully to the conquest.

Sometimes it's a sacrifice, so let's get practical. It might mean releasing a romantic relationship because it isn't established on a godly foundation. It might mean accepting the awkwardness of not knowing the latest and greatest shows on TV because your passion and attention are captured by another culture. It might mean turning down a lucrative business opportunity in order to take a missions trip. But the New Rebellion worshiper discovers that worship is its own reward.

Worship

the point

To join this worshiping invasion of planet Earth costs nothing but requires everything. You don't have to be good enough, smart enough, or popular enough—Jesus took care of all that on the cross. The community of God that is gathering to shake the world will be focused, passionate, and utterly given over to the glory of God's Kingdom. Your energy and affection belong to Him and are gladly yielded to His good intentions.

the talk

All of history is moving toward one great goal, the white-hot worship of God and his Son among all the peoples of the earth. Missions exist because worship doesn't.

JOHN PIPER

Sometimes You're further than the moon; sometimes You're closer than my skin; and You surround me like a winter fog . . . You've come and burned me with a kiss.

MARTIN SMITH

The central paradigm . . . is that our worship of God either affirms or contradicts our message about God.

SALLY MORGENTHALER

Why, then, do we worry about recession, cartels, changes in world leadership, and ungodliness? Can they stop God from presenting to this world a Church which is glorious, spotless, and full of the power of God?

JUDSON CORNWALL

the word

I beg you to offer your lives as a living sacrifice to him. Your offering must be only for God and pleasing to him, which is the spiritual way for you to worship. Do not change yourselves to be like the people of this world, but be changed within by a new way of thinking.

Romans 12:1–2 NCV

The hour is coming, and now is, when the true worshipers will worship the Father in spirit and truth; for the Father is seeking such to worship Him. God is Spirit, and those who worship Him must worship in spirit and truth.

John 4:23–24 NKJV

"Holy, holy, holy is the Lord God Almighty. He was, he is, and he is coming." These living creatures give glory, honor, and thanks to the One who sits on the throne, who lives forever and ever. Then the twenty-four elders bow down before the One who sits on the throne, and they worship him who lives forever and ever.

Revelation 4:8–10 NCV

All nations whom You have made shall come and worship before You, O Lord, and shall glorify Your name. For You are great, and do wondrous things; You alone are God.

Psalm 86:9–10 NKJV

When the trumpeters and singers were as one, to make one sound to be heard in praising and thanking the LORD, and when they lifted up their voice with the trumpets and cymbals and instruments of music, and praised the LORD, saying: "For He is good, for His mercy endures forever," that the house, the house of the LORD, was filled with a cloud, so that the priests could not continue ministering because of the cloud; for the glory of the LORD filled the house of God.

2 Chronicles 5:13–14 NKJV

Worship

19

the worship tools

Read it . . .

The Air I Breathe
Louie Giglio
Worship as life.

Blended Worship
Robert Webber
Strategies for combining traditional and contemporary forms.

Exploring Worship
Bob Sorge
The modern classic on the theology and practice of worship.

For the Audience of One
Mike Pilavachi
A Godward view of 24/7 worship.

A Lifestyle of Worship
David Morris
Living out your worship every day.

The New Worship
Barry Liesch
Fresh perspectives on worship planning and practice, history, theology, and spiritual formation.

The Unquenchable Worshipper
Matt Redman
A passionate call to a first-love worship.

Worship Evangelism
Sally Morgenthaler
Drawing people to God through non-religious worship.

Surf it . . .

www.integritymusic.com
Music, forums, events, and resources.

www.passionnow.org
Events and resources to light a fire in university students.

www.switchfoot.com
Cool site for the band Switchfoot.

www.worshiptogether.com
An online worship community.

Hear it . . .

Adoration, Newsboys

Arriving, Chris Tomlin

Enter the Worship Circle, Blue Renaissance

Here I Am to Worship, Tim Hughes

Illuminate, David Crowder Band

United: More Than Life, Hillsong

Worship, Michael W. Smith

Do it . . .

24/7 worship and prayer at the *International House of Prayer* in Kansas City, www.ihop.org.

24/7 worship and prayer at the *World Prayer Center in Colorado Springs*, www.theworldprayercenter.org.

TOP TEN

The Top Ten Ways to Rebel Against Idols

10 Give the best part of your day, not your leftovers, to being with God.

9 Volunteer one Saturday morning at your local homeless shelter this month.

8 Pass up the hundred-dollar tennis shoes for something comfortable and affordable.

7 Pray specifically for the people in your sphere of influence.

6 Feed your soul with Kingdom-affirming images from television, music, and movies.

5 Take a foreign-missions trip this year.

4 Enjoy sports, but don't overdose.

3 Build a healthy body instead of a glamorous image.

2 Develop your spiritual gifts as intentionally as your career.

1 Make it your lifelong quest to know yourself and to know God!

The Question

What occupies the greatest amount of time, thinking, and emotional energy in your life?

The tough reality is that people usually judge others by their actions, and yet they judge themselves by their intentions. The result is a distance—sometimes larger, sometimes smaller—between the person you think you are and the person you actually are.

Christ-followers want Jesus to be the center of their universe, the sun around which their lives orbit. But that central place is challenged by many impostors, many false gods that draw attention and affection after their own empty promises. What is at stake is nothing less than your worship.

You need to be brutally honest with yourself and consider where your mind settles when nothing else is occupying its attention. Is there something that sucks up all your free time and energy? And the all-important query: Is whatever dominates your mind born of God's Kingdom? Or is it characterized by the empty and temporary shell of this world's system?

It isn't that you shouldn't enjoy simple pleasures—good music, a fun movie, eating with friends, or a favorite hobby. But if your life is defined by those things, then you will be impotent as a world-changer. The New Rebellion worshipers keep first things first—they give the first and best of themselves to God and His interests, and, as a result, they live in such a way as to make a Kingdom impact upon the world.

Only God is worth your greatest loyalty. Only God deserves the praise of your life. And it is your life that will

The New Rebellion worshipers keep first things first—they give the first and best of themselves to God and His interests, and, as a result, they live in such a way as to make a Kingdom impact upon the world.

show, more than your words, who or what is your greatest love. So go ahead. Rebel against all those false gods, and go for the real adventure of worshiping God alone with all that you are and all that you do. You won't be disappointed.

Love the Lord your God with all your heart, all your soul, all your mind, and all your strength.
Mark 12:30 NCV

A Wildfire of Truth and Passion

CHARLES WESLEY

1707–1788

Love divine, all loves excelling, joy of heaven, to earth come down; fix in us thy humble dwelling; all thy faithful mercies crown! Jesus, thou art all compassion, pure, unbounded love thou art; visit us with thy salvation; enter every trembling heart.

Charles Wesley, 1747

Charles, along with his better-known brother, John, broke upon the scene in eighteenth-century England with a position of sheer rebellion. In the midst of a pervasive religious view that emphasized the complete wickedness of men and women and a limited salvation that extended only to the elect—those chosen by God—those passionate brothers led a revolt of grace.

Though both were ordained Anglican priests, John was the preacher and the more public figure, while Charles unleashed a tidal wave of worship through hymns and poetry—literally hundreds of hymns and thousands of poems. He was one of the most prolific English poets of all time.

The radical soul of Charles was birthed out of great personal struggle and self-doubt. After a missionary stint in the new colony of Georgia, the spiritual insights of Kezie, his younger sister, greatly affected him, and he wrote in his journal: "By degrees the Spirit of God chased away the darkness of my unbelief. I found myself convinced . . . I saw that by faith I stood."

And stand he did. Together with his brother John and the preacher George Whitefield, Charles sparked a revelation of God's free grace that was seeded into the human heart and available to all. Even while church officials barred them from English pulpits, crowds of up to twenty-five thousand would gather outdoors to be influenced by the radical nature of this young and zealous worshiper. A movement had begun. And it would help instigate the revival known as the First Great Awakening across the ocean in America.

Even though this movement became known as Methodism, many Methodists often found themselves unwilling to sing many of Charles's hymns. Why? The depth of passion contained in his lyrics felt too profound, too intimate, and too radical for some with lesser fire in their souls. This was a man who burned. As his brother put it, "Catch on fire with enthusiasm, and people will come for miles to watch you burn!"

The fiery heart of Charles Wesley changed his world as well as yours.

wisdom from the past

A Vocal Rebel

REBECCA ST. JAMES
Singer

To experience all the freedom and joy God has in store for you, you can't coast or stop. None of us can. We must keep moving by allowing God to empower us, and He does that by changing us . . . Through discovering and pursuing our God-given purpose, we stay on track and away from distractions that take our focus off of Him and that rob us of the power He offers.

from SHE by Rebecca St. James

Rebecca, whose real name is Rebecca Jean Smallbone, was just a regular Aussie girl in 1991 when she relocated to the United States, but could she ever sing! As a young teenager, Rebecca decided to rebel. Fortunately, she rebelled against the right stuff and chose to live a life of radical obedience to Christ.

Her driving hunger for God led her to weave her passion into lyrics, lyrics that took America by storm several years later when her second album—with the simple title *God*—took off. The heart cry of this New Rebellion worshiper lies thick in the gripping lines of her songs.

"Rebecca's commitment to God and His Word have clearly been the central tenets of her music and ministry, and I think that's the main reason for her success and her popularity," said Mark Moring of *Campus Life* magazine. "Sure, her music is hip and innovative, but it's her underlying commitment to Christ and her unabashed proclamation of God's love that primarily attract the listener."

One of the ways in which Rebecca confronts this world's system is by speaking out for sexual purity among young people. There are few things that fracture the souls of men and women more than sexual immorality. Scripture says that "every sin that a man does is outside the body, but he who commits sexual immorality sins against his own body" (1 Corinthians 6:18 NKJV). This radical singer invites people everywhere to say no to the lies of this world and to be fully abandoned to God.

Of course, God redeems and heals every kind of sin, including sexual sin, but the New Rebellion generation rises up to call young people to a new vision of personal purity so that they can impact this world as worshiping warriors for God.

vital stats

- Born: July 26, 1977

- First album at age 14

- Favorite verse: Acts 20:24: "My life is worth nothing unless I use it for doing the work assigned me by the Lord Jesus—the work of telling others the Good News about God's wonderful kindness and love" (NLT).

- Impacted greatly by a missions trip to Romania

- Loves to swing dance, swim, and read Christian fiction

wisdom from the now

When you do things, do not let selfishness or pride be your guide. Instead, be humble and give more honor to others than to yourselves.

Philippians 2:3 NCV

Warring for Another

Relationships are the currency of God's Kingdom. Nothing else is as valuable in the culture of heaven as our intimate connection to God and one another. If this is true, then a passion for thriving, healthy relationships must dominate the vision of every Christ-follower.

The term "relationship" covers a broad sweep of life, but this chapter will focus on the intimate friendships in your life—the one, two, or three people who know you best. It may be a romantic relationship or it may not. But it's where your soul goes deep.

Depth and commitment are what separate "hanging out" from life-transforming interdependence. Friendship is a commitment forged in the heat of battle. And until your relationship is tested by conflict, you don't really know what you have. Lasting friendships use every obstacle as a means to know each other deeply and reinforce an enduring commitment to each other's good.

Relationships

the buzz

There is nothing that our world needs more than good relationships, and perhaps nothing defines our world more than the brokenness of its relationships. Against this trend, the New Rebellion issues a defining truth: People will always be more important than projects. This may sound self-evident, but it isn't. Today's culture is consumed with production and evaluates People on their ability to generate excellent work, not on their ability to nurture excellent relationships. There is no part of society that is not affected by the elevation of performance at the expense of personal intimacy.

When you do things, do not let selfishness or pride be your guide. Instead, be humble and give more honor to others than to yourselves.

Philippians 2:3 NCV

Even the church bears the mark of this misguided value structure with ever-increasing emphasis on organizational structures for ministry rather than on organic, spontaneous connections of people ministering to one another. Friendships drift into functional partnerships instead of the actual sharing of life. Into this vacuum of disassociated souls, the New Rebellion raises a vision once again for authentic community.

How do you build authentic relationships? Quality time is the usual answer, and that's half right. It takes both quality and quantity, however, to get into the cracks and chinks of life. To get past the superficial. To take off your masks and be real.

Building relationships that can go the distance combines the resource of time with the skill of intention. Relationships can't be rushed any more than you can hurry along the blooming of a flower. Both require adequate time and adequate care. Care comes from being intentional—using your time with your friends to deepen your understanding of one another, to touch the hidden places of the soul, and to contribute out of your own soul. Contribute what? Wisdom, perspective, solidarity, your very presence. Your soul's contribution will be many things.

Real relationships are built when you guard your brother's back and know that he has yours. When you know that your failures, your triumphs, and your destiny are owned and carried by your closest friends. This is the climate that empowers growth and transformation, whether the context is marriage or friendship or church.

> Building relation-ships that can go the distance combines the resource of time with the skill of intention.
>
>

God is raising the bar for the expression of His relational vision in the earth. He is releasing men and women today who are passionate about con-nection—about spiritual intimacy with Him and spiritual interdependency with one another. Lone rangers are in the past. Superstars and celebrities are passé. Heaven values relationship. God's work in the earth requires it. Your destiny mandates it. Are you prepared to reach for true relationships in your life? The rewards are well worth your investment.

Relationships

the insight

King Saul's son Jonathan is nearly always mentioned in the same breath with his friend David. But Jonathan experienced another compelling friendship—a bond built not in the palace but on the battlefield.

Saul's "army" was camped out, trying to defend themselves against the marauding Philistines (see 1 Samuel 14). But it wasn't much of an army. Jonathan and Saul were the only ones who even owned a sword or spear; the rest were probably carrying axes and pitchforks. Fear and desperation were in the air. Except in two hearts.

> True friendship has a redemptive power that surpasses the relationship itself and moves the entire community toward its destiny.

Jonathan was itching for a fight and anxious for God to get some recognition. He spoke in low tones to the soldier who carried his armor, "Come with me," and together they sneaked out of camp. As they headed toward an outpost of enemy soldiers camped up on a cliff, Jonathan explained his plan—if you could call it a plan.

"Come on now, let's go across to these uncircumcised pagans. Maybe GOD will work for us. There's no rule that says GOD can only deliver by using a big army. No one can stop GOD from saving when he sets his mind to it" (verse 6 MSG). Now, you've got to love his buddy's reply. There were a couple dozen or more enemy soldiers in the outpost; he didn't even have a sword. But with absolute confidence he answered Jonathan, "Go ahead. Do what you think best. I'm with you all the way" (verse 7 MSG).

So as their enemies talked trash over exactly how they planned to kill them, those two courageous warriors did a little mountain climbing. Once they reached the top, they brushed themselves off, caught their breath, and prepared to fight. It must have been a scene to rival William Wallace's battle at Stirling in *Braveheart*!

They merged into a seamless unity that was astounding, and their enemies began to fall. Jonathan wounded one and turned to block a blow from another. Jonathan's comrade-in-arms dispatched the first and blocked a spear thrust toward Jonathan. Their oneness of purpose was unstoppable, their courage unshakable as they danced destruction upon their invaders.

This solitary act of boldness left twenty men dead before the rest bolted. Through it, God incited a panic that infected the entire Philistine army so that *they* bolted—with the Israelites in hot pursuit! True friendship has a redemptive power that surpasses the relationship itself and moves the entire community toward its destiny.

Relationships

the point

Don't think that you don't face an equally hostile enemy. And don't think that you can survive your spiritual enemy—much less put him to flight—without a few relationships that are utterly committed to your good. Relationships with friends, friends in whom you have invested during peaceful times and who prove themselves in the hard times. The bonds that are established in your life-and-death struggles are ones that will go the distance and last a lifetime.

the talk

You will find as you look back upon your life that the moments when you have truly lived are the moments when you have done things in the spirit of love.

HENRY DRUMMOND

A friend hears the song in my heart and sings it to me when my memory fails.

ANONYMOUS

I want to trip inside your head, spend the day there . . . To hear the things you haven't said and see what you might see.

PAUL HEWSON, AKA BONO

Don't marry the person you think you can live with; marry only the individual you think you can't live without.

JAMES DOBSON

Tears shed for self are tears of weakness, but tears shed for others are a sign of strength.

BILLY GRAHAM

the word

Behold, how good and how pleasant it is for brethren to dwell together in unity! . . . It is like the dew of Hermon, descending upon the mountains of Zion; for there the LORD commanded the blessing—life forevermore.

Psalm 133:1, 3 NKJV

Just as lotions and fragrance give sensual delight, a sweet friendship refreshes the soul.

Proverbs 27:9 MSG

People's thoughts can be like a deep well, but someone with understanding can find the wisdom there.

Proverbs 20:5 NCV

Husbands, love your wives, just as Christ also loved the church and gave Himself for her, that He might sanctify and cleanse her with the washing of water by the word.

Ephesians 5:25–26 NKJV

The greatest love a person can show is to die for his friends.

John 15:13 NCV

Relationships

the relationship tools

Read it . . .

Bonding: Relationships in the Image of God
Dr. Donald M. Joy
God's design for intimacy and its effects upon the family.

Boundaries
Dr. Henry Cloud and Dr. John Townsend
Essential skills for healthy relationships.

The Healing Path
Dan Allender
Chapter 12 is worth the cost of the book!

Her Hand in Marriage: Biblical Courtship in the Modern World
Douglas Wilson
An alternative to the traditional dating scene.

How to Really Love Your Child
Dr. Ross Campbell
The simplest and most powerful tools for rearing children.

In the Company of Women
Dr. Brenda Hunter
A refreshing look at women's friendships.

Marriage on the Rock
Jimmy Evans
A practical and readable guidebook for marriage.

Surf it . . .

www.campuslife.net
Relational resources for high school and college.

www.christianitytoday.com/marriage
Articles and resources for healthy marriages.

www.fltoday.org
Family Life Today—tools for effective family relationships.

www.soulcare.com
Spiritual practices for authentic growth.

Hear it . . .

All About Love, Steven Curtis Chapman

All Things New, Watermark

Brave, Nicole Nordeman

Conversations, Sara Groves

Everyone's Beautiful, Waterdeep

Do it . . .

Life renewal for fathers and sons at **Sonwaker Adventures,** www.sonwaker.com.

Weekend to Remember marriage seminar, www.fltoday.org.

Experience relational conferences by **Henry Cloud and John Townsend** at www.cloudtownsend.com.

TOP TEN

The Top Ten Ways to "Win Friends and Influence People"

10   Respect other people's time, space, and values.

9   Listen beyond words to someone's heart.

8   Ask questions in order to get to know someone.

7   Be vulnerable with the people closest to you.

6   Make time for people, not just projects.

5   Spend time in prayer with the people you love.

4   Go beyond chitchat to real-life issues.

3   Know your friends' real dreams and intimidations.

2   Take a road trip to build a friendship.

1   Have fun together in spontaneous ways.

> We are so obsessed with doing that we have no time
> and no imagination left for being. As a result, men
> are valued not for what they are but for what they do
> or what they have—for their usefulness.
>
> **Thomas Merton**

The Question

Do your family and friends feel elevated by your presence and encouraged by your interactions?

The intersection of two souls always has a ripple effect. Every word is like a stone tossed in the water—long after the rock disappears, its impact is felt. And so it is with every relational exchange. Which is good cause to consider both the weight and the direction of your presence with friends. Are they elevated or dissipated after time with you? Encouraged or discouraged?

Author Brent Curtis wrote this: "Let people feel the weight of who you are . . . and let them deal with it." In other words, be the real you even if the real you rocks people's boats. Still, the "real you" can be either a positive or a negative influence on others, drawing people toward the beauty of God in you or, alternately, pushing them away. People have to deal with who you are, so what is it that you are leaving in your wake for people to deal with?

Another way to phrase the question: Are you a giver or a taker? Some people are so emotionally bankrupt that they suck every ounce of life and energy out of you in a matter of minutes. Are you that person? On the other hand, there are those rare souls who seem to emanate an almost visible light of joy, whose affection and genuine caring are an instant salve to troubled minds. Are you that person?

> Be the real you even if the real you rocks people's boats.

There is one source of life: Jesus. When all of your actions and words are anchored in His life, then you are a carrier of that life and become life to all you encounter. How powerful your relationships then become. What if you prayed and asked God for a specific word of encouragement for a friend before you saw them? Wow, how life-giving you would be! As a godly rebel, this is your destiny.

Let people feel the weight
of who you are . . . and let
them deal with it.
Brent Curtis

Brilliance Gone Mad?

DIETRICH BONHOEFFER
1906–1945

It is easily forgotten that the fellowship of Christian [friends] is a gift of grace, a gift of the Kingdom of God that any day may be taken from us, that the time that still separates us from utter loneliness may be brief indeed.

Dietrich Bonhoeffer

"Christianity means community through Jesus Christ and in Jesus Christ. No Christian community is more or less than this. Whether it be a brief, single encounter or the daily fellowship of years, Christian community is only this. We belong to one another only through and in Jesus Christ." These words were penned by Dietrich Bonhoeffer in his book *Life Together*.

Bonhoeffer had unique insight into the relational beauty and spiritual neccesity of living life integrated with Christian friends and family. He believed that reading the Bible together, worshiping together, and sharing stories together were not just for congregational settings; he believed that these activities were necessary for small, intimate interactions.

It wasn't mere theory for this courageous soul: In the spring of 1935, he took leadership of a small seminary by the Baltic Sea, not only to teach theology to prospective ministers, but also to actually live out his vision for Christian community. In the midst of these men and women, Bonhoeffer explored what it meant to live out one's faith in intentional relationship, and he wrote his best-known works.

Bonhoeffer was an integrator. Theology was never meant to be compartmentalized off into the realm of the intellect. Theology was meant to be lived—to be demonstrated in the eating, interacting, and sleeping of the real world. Plus, belief had tremendous social and political ramifications. Within a few years of his seminary experiment in community, he became involved with the Abwehr resistance circle, which arose in opposition to national socialism, the Nazi agenda, and the persecution of the Jews. The personal integrity of this man moved him into a group of relationships focused around a mission—the overthrow of Hitler. After a failed assassination attempt on the führer, Dietrich was hanged in a concentration camp at the age of thirty-nine, but his legacy of communal theology lives on.

wisdom from the past

One of life's greatest tragedies
is a person with a 10-by-12
capacity and a two-by-four soul.
Dr. Kenneth Hildebrand

Where Are You Headed?

Destiny could be considered a selfish pursuit. But it isn't.

Destiny is all about God's story—a story that began at Creation and will one day be unfurled in all its amazing dimensions. Into God's story breaks your story, and that is the reason for destiny. You are no accident, you are no awkward appendage to God's plan; you are an essential component of His purpose in the world.

Because of this, you need to understand your place in the story. And that place is not a secret. Most people—even many Christ-followers—blunder their way through life without ever really tapping into their divine destinies. That is tragic and unnecessary since God is actively speaking to His people all the time. But you have to listen.

After Jesus told stories, He would frequently ask, "Are you listening to Me? Really listening?" To fulfill your destiny, you have to pay attention.

Destiny

the buzz

Why is it that destiny often seems to hang out there and not move closer to reality? Well, the first reason has already been mentioned—many people merely push ahead, letting life shape their purposes on its own terms. This will absolutely frustrate your destiny. Others, however, do pay attention and are pursuing the pieces of destiny that have come from God.

Destiny has several components: It is *progressive*, it is *communal*, and it contains *strategic pauses*.

Progressive. First, destiny does not usually emerge in one lump deposit. Rather, God speaks out what you need to hear when you need to hear it. What's important is that you act on what you hear, even if it cuts across what seems "normal" or conventional. The world is not changed by the normal and conventional, is it?!

Wherever your treasure is, there your heart and thoughts will also be.

Matthew 6:21 NLT

Psalm 119:105 says that God's word is a light to your path. Two observations: God's word is not just the Scriptures. While the Bible is the standard for understanding all other "words," God speaks through many, many things—people, situations, movies, books, music, spiritual leaders, and so forth. Listen and look for His voice in every facet of your daily life.

Communal. The second observation is that the light that emerges from God's words usually shines just as far as you need to see. You will catch glimmers and glimpses of shapes down the path, but the clarity for faith and obedience falls upon the next couple of steps. Take those. Then God will illuminate the next section of the path.

In addition to being progressive, destiny is communal. God rarely speaks His chosen future into an isolated heart. Destiny is discovered and interpreted within a spiritual community. Not only that, but destiny is meant to be lived out within community. Wisdom, discernment, courage, and partnership—all essential qualities for following your destiny—are available to you only within the core relationships of family and faith. Build these relationships intentionally.

> **D**estiny has several components: It is *progressive*, it is *communal*, and it contains *strategic pauses*.

Contains strategic pauses. A third quality of destiny involves seasons of waiting. These are often frustrating and disorienting, but they need not be. Waiting has always been an essential part of God's preparation for His people of destiny. You will be hard-pressed to find a key biblical figure who did not experience a notable time of pause.

So what do you do when God waits? You embrace the moment, look for opportunities of equipping, and lean into His trusted arms. Pursue the pieces of destiny that are available, even if they seem insignificant, and never let go of your calling. "Do not cast away your confidence, which has great reward" (Hebrews 10:35 NKJV).

Destiny

the insight

If there was ever a man of startling destiny, it was Joseph. Yep, the guy with the Technicolor coat (see Genesis 37–50). As son number twelve, there wasn't a whole lot expected of Joseph. In that day, son number one got all the breaks—and the inheritance. Still, his father, Jacob, did love Joseph more than all his brothers. Which became a big problem.

> Joseph trusted and prayed and reached for purpose in his dismal surroundings. That resilience continually brought him recognition and favor.

Destiny grabbed Joseph early with dreams—literal dreams—of grandeur that he would be raised to prominence within his family. Such prominence that all his siblings and even his own mother and father would venerate him. Ever confident and even cocky, Joseph didn't mind flaunting his dreams among his brothers. In reply, they took him by force and sold him into slavery.

Destiny took an abrupt turn.

For thirteen long years, Joseph endured the absolute antithesis of his God-given destiny and, as a result, had many opportunities to give up on it and throw his dreams away in bitterness. You, too, will have such opportunities. The fragments of destiny that you cling to will be tested by time, by silence, and by suffering. *Whoa, that's not the happy news I was looking for*, you might think.

Joseph's test of time was so keen that hundreds of years later, King David wrote about it: "Until the time that his word came to pass, the word of the LORD tested him [Joseph]" (Psalm 105:19 NASB). His destiny hung over him like a banner of shame, even if no one could see it but himself. It burned under him like an oven, slow-roasting his soul.

The silence of God taunted him in the recesses of a prison cell. Falsely accused. Reputation marred. Prospects zero. Still, Joseph trusted and prayed and reached for purpose in his dismal surroundings. That resilience continually brought him recognition and favor. Because silence does not mean absence. If you have not yet experienced the silence of God, don't worry. You will. But He will never leave you or throw away your destiny. Only you can throw away your destiny, but you don't want to do that.

Joseph refused to get bitter, refused to relinquish his character, and refused to doubt God's good intention toward him. Those choices were so potent that they eventually propelled his destiny into reality and became the qualifying forces that actually enabled him to be the ruler he was meant to be.

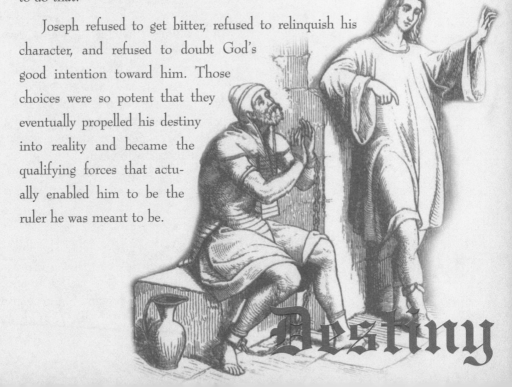

Destiny

the point

An intriguing verse in Hebrews says that "though he was God's Son, [Jesus] learned trusting-obedience by what he suffered, just as we do" (5:8 MSG). In a way that's hard to fully grasp, the sufferings of Jesus qualified Him for His destiny. And it's no different for you. Pain tests and highlights what's inside people, and what's inside comes out. Allow your pain to bring forth the depth of character that qualifies you for your destiny.

the talk

God has created me to do him some definite service; he has committed some work to me which he has not committed to another. I have my mission.

JOHN HENRY NEWMAN

We are prepared to serve the Lord only by sacrifice. We are fit for the work of God only when we have wept over it, prayed about it, and then we are enabled by Him to tackle the job that needs to be done. May God give to us hearts that bleed, eyes that are wide open to see, minds that are clear to interpret God's purposes, wills that are obedient, and a determination that is utterly unflinching as we set about the tasks He would have us do.

ALAN REDPATH

Be inspired with the belief that life is a great and noble calling; not a mean and groveling thing that we are to shuffle through as we can, but an elevated and lofty destiny.

WILLIAM E. GLADSTONE

the word

Where there is no vision, the people are unrestrained, but happy is he who keeps the law.

Proverbs 29:18 NASB

To everyone who has, more will be given, and he will have abundance . . . When the Son of Man comes in His glory, and all the holy angels with Him, then He will sit on the throne of His glory. All the nations will be gathered before Him, and He will separate them one from another, as a shepherd divides his sheep from the goats. And He will set the sheep on His right hand, but the goats on the left. Then the King will say to those on His right hand, "Come, you blessed of My Father, inherit the kingdom prepared for you from the foundation of the world."

Matthew 25:29, 31–34 NKJV

God is in charge of deciding human destiny.

James 4:12 MSG

David, after he had served his own generation by the will of God, fell asleep, [and] was buried with his fathers.

Acts 13:36 NKJV

[The Holy Spirit] knows us far better than we know ourselves, knows our pregnant condition, and keeps us present before God. That's why we can be so sure that every detail in our lives of love for God is worked into something good. God knew what he was doing from the very beginning. He decided from the outset to shape the lives of those who love him along the same lines as the life of his Son. The Son stands first in the line of humanity he restored. We see the original and intended shape of our lives there in him.

Romans 8:27–29 MSG

Destiny

1 the destiny tools

Read it . . .

The Blessing
Gary Smalley and John Trent
Release blessing up and down the generations.

The Dream Giver
Bruce Wilkinson
Following your God-given destiny.

Chasing God, Serving Man
Tommy Tenney
Merging passion for God and compassion for others.

Fatal Distractions
Joyce Rodgers
Uncover the roadblocks that keep you from destiny.

Possessing Your Inheritance
Chuck Pierce and Rebecca Systema
Becoming the person God fully intended you to be.

Sacred Romance
John Eldredge and Brent Curtis
You were made for more!

When God Waits
Jerome Daley
Understanding your strategic seasons of life.

Women: God's Secret Weapon
Ed Silvoso
Validating God's destiny for women.

Surf it . . .

www.chosengeneration.cc
A Christian youth group in Miami serving you.

www.morningstarministries.org
Conferences and resources to promote destiny.

www.team-swap.com
Independent forum for swapping stories of faith.

www.youthfire.com
Youth-based portal with forums, etc.

Hear it . . .

The Beautiful Letdown, Switchfoot
Cross Seekers, Various
Cutting Edge, Delirious
Destiny, The Katinas
Mary Mary, Mary Mary
Reaching, LaRue
The Way I Am, Jennifer Knapp

Do it . . .

Battle Cry events, Acquire the Fire, youth destiny,
www.acquirethefire.com.

LifeChange Seminars, conquer your past, newchurch2002.tripod.com/LifeChange.

TOP TEN

The Top Ten Ways to Make Good Decisions

10 Invite counsel from trusted people within your spiritual community.

9 Let God reshape or amplify the inherent desires of your heart.

8 Look for your story inside of God's story throughout the Bible.

7 Pay attention to God's still, small whisper.

6 When unsure or confused, wait for the peace.

5 Pursue the vision God has given until more comes.

4 If God isn't speaking, wait.

3 Look for God to confirm His will in several ways.

2 Capitalize on both the mistakes and the victories of the past.

1 Listen constantly, trust unceasingly, act boldly.

The Question

Do you believe that God has a plan for your life and that if you stay close to Him, He will make it happen?

Either destiny is a myth of human manufacturing, a sort of wish-fulfillment dynamic, or it is the result of a God who is both good *and* strong. If it is the former, then no one profits from talk of destiny. If it is the latter, then no decision you make in life must fail to reflect that larger understanding.

If God is not fundamentally good—which pain sometimes bends you toward believing on a subconscious level—then destiny is suspect. *If* God is good, but not powerful, then His intentions toward you are wonderful, but He cannot be trusted to deliver on His promises. But if God is both good *and* strong, then there is no disappointment, no obstacle, no delay that can short-circuit your destiny.

And if you can trust the testimony of King David, he said this: "God has spoken plainly, and I have heard it many times: Power, O God, belongs to you; unfailing love, O Lord, is yours" (Psalm 62:11–12 NLT). Good and strong, you win.

So, is your destiny a done deal, then? Well, actually, no. There is the matter of walking it out, by faith, together with Him. Together in relationship. Your destiny exists, sure and secure, but you must stick close by Him—to hear His heart, to know His timing, and to live it out within community. Community with Him and community with others.

If God is both good and strong, then there is no disappointment, no obstacle, no delay that can short-circuit your destiny.

Destiny does not fulfill itself. But if you stay tucked in with God, He will bring it to completion. And it will be a beautiful thing.

There has never been the slightest doubt in my mind that the God who started this great work in you would keep at it and bring it to a flourishing finish on the very day Christ Jesus appears.
Philippians 1:6 MSG

"I Will Die for My Faith"

CASSIE RENE BERNALL

1982–1999

Modern-Day Martyr

Cassie's story has touched me time and time again. The faith is just incredible. I was once told everyone dies, but not everyone lives. I will always remember her courage and faith and will tell her story to my children. I wait for the day to meet this incredible lady.

Tim Flannery, third-base coach, San Diego Padres

"I will die for my faith. It's the least I can do for Christ dying for me." These words of destiny came from Cassie's own mouth. And on April 20, 1999, this courageous seventeen-year-old fulfilled her destiny by looking into the face of a gunman. Two students at Columbine High School in Littleton, Colorado, went on a killing rampage that eventually ended in the deaths of twelve students, one teacher, and the killers themselves. In the high school library, the killer cornered Cassie and challenged her, "Do you believe in God?" A pause . . . then "Yes, I believe in God." With the callous reply of "Why?" he pulled the trigger and instantly ended Cassie's life.

Years earlier, Cassie had been a troubled girl, experimenting with drugs, toying with the occult, on numerous occasions threatening to kill herself or run away. But one spring, Cassie was invited by a friend to a church camp in Estes Park. The presence of God, particularly in the singing, finally broke through the shell that encrusted her soul, and she broke. Along with other kids, Cassie poured out her heart to God, confessing a long string of bad decisions and taking responsibility for her past choices.

Her parents were shocked when she returned. In an unemotional, straightforward way, she declared, "Mom, I've totally changed. I know you are not going to believe it, but I'll prove it to you." And she did. It wasn't an overnight transformation, but the turning point was real and began a gradual process of spiritual growth and a new inner life.

Martyrdom is a spiritual reality that every Christ-follower experiences at one level—it is the choice to die to a self-centered life and choose a destiny shaped by God. For two years, Cassie made those choices . . . until one day that choice propelled her directly into the embrace of Jesus.

The morning Cassie was killed, she handed this note to a friend: "Honestly, I want to live completely for God; it's hard and scary but totally worth it."

During those times you sit in the presence of God and your heart sighs for him, what is it you are sighing for? Understand that your sigh originated in his heart.

Graham Cooke

Near the Heart of God

You are hard-wired to yearn for intimacy. The very fabric of every man's and every woman's soul longs to know another . . . and to be known in return. Years and years of neglect or isolation can dull that yearning, but cannot extinguish the cry of the human heart—*Know me and love me!*

God's design would be a cruel hoax if He did not intend to completely satisfy that yearning. But of course He does. And so He speaks these incredible words of invitation: *Come close to Me . . . at your first step, at even the hint of movement, I will dash to your side and be your most intimate friend.* And when His affection wraps around you like the warmth of a blazing fire, you can almost hear your soul sigh with relief. *Yes, I am loved beyond belief.*

Intimacy

57

the buzz

Theology has always grappled to reconcile many of the paradoxes of God. Unfortunately—or fortunately—the paradoxes cannot be solved by rational efforts; they can only be accepted in awe and gratitude. God's ways are so beyond human grasp that people will always marvel and be mystified by them. If the mystery ever fades into calculated constructs of human wisdom, then theology will have failed and truth will have slipped through, eluding the effort to reduce the divine to malleable components.

For example, the nature of God is so fundamentally different from your nature that the word *holiness* was created to describe it. At the same time, God is determined to come into intimate relationship with His children, and so He makes Himself accessible to the cry of any person's heart, no matter how down and out he is. The fact that both qualities—His holiness and His nearness—are simultaneously true mystifies the mind.

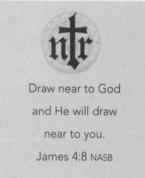

Draw near to God
and He will draw
near to you.
James 4:8 NASB

But not the heart. The New Rebellion generation consists of those radical souls (of any age) who are not content to worship from afar, not satisfied to contemplate God's holiness from a distance but are compelled to know God as a heart friend. Some worry that such familiarity will breed contempt, but those who really know Him know that it never can. The closer you draw to Him, the closer He draws to you. And the closer you get, the more fascinating and frightening and wonderfully comforting His nature becomes.

Just as you draw close in human relationships through time and focus, you also move toward Jesus in the same manner. There are places of intimacy that are simply not accessible without adequate time to go there. Of course, all your days and hours and minutes belong to Him, and the man or woman of intimacy will live in a constant connection with God. But there are specific times to be purposeful, to direct your full attention to the pursuit and enjoyment of God.

> The nature of God is so fundamentally different from your nature that the word *holiness* was created to describe it.
>
>

It is important to understand that intentionality is not the same as being structured. There is a place for strategic structure—chapters in the Bible to read, specific intercession for others, and so forth—but there is also a place for strategic nonstructure. Certain facets of intimacy only open up as you allow God to lead you into new places of His heart or yours. Find time to simply hang out with God: Think about your life from His perspective. Listen for His whispers. Ponder what He is teaching you through your current circumstances. These are some ways intimacy is created.

Intimacy

the insight

Being intimate with God. Sounds daunting. Feelings of unworthiness . . . shadows of past failures. Is such a thing really accessible? And if so, wouldn't it just be for the spiritual elite? Yes, it is accessible. No, it isn't just for monks and nuns. Intimacy is by invitation, and you have been invited.

Read God's own words: "You are no longer a slave, but a son; and if a son, then an heir through God" (Galatians 4:7 HCSB). Put your name in there—*you* are no longer a slave who barely made the cut and was grudgingly accepted into the Kingdom. You are a son or daughter of the Most High. You are legitimate, the object of immeasurable affection, the prize of God's passion. And, if that isn't enough, you won a priceless inheritance, and that inheritance is intimacy. Of all the riches God gives, His greatest offer is Himself.

> **Y**our ultimate destiny in God is the intimacy of two lovers.
>
>

"I no longer call you servants, because a servant does not know his master's business. Instead, I have called you friends" (John 15:15 NIV).

But God's kids are frequently reluctant to believe their good fortune. *Maybe I'm not a slave*, they think, *but I'm still a servant. My job is just to do what I'm told, and then maybe He will like me.* But God ups the ante: "You're not a slave. You're not merely a servant. Not only are you My child, but I call you My friend!"

What's the difference between a child and a friend? Age. Growth and maturity. As children grow up into adults, the dynamic changes from simple obedience toward actual friendship. And you, too, are invited to "grow up" into friendship with your heavenly Father. How many of God's children ever make that transition? Will you be one? The door is open, and He invites you to know His deepest heart! Amazing but true.

But even friendship isn't intimate enough for your destiny in God. Paul laid it out: "'A man leaves his father and mother and is joined to his wife, and the two are united into one.' This is a great mystery, but it is an illustration of the way Christ and the church are one" (Ephesians 5:31–32 NLT). Your ultimate destiny in God is the intimacy of two lovers. You wouldn't dare believe it if He hadn't said it Himself.

Intimacy

the point

Have you ever seen yourself in the Song of Solomon? Have you ever read the words "You are altogether desirable," and heard Jesus whispering them into your heart? Could Jesus really become your lover, your truest friend, your safest confidant? Dare to venture into the most intimate chambers with King Solomon and his bride; see if you can find yourself there, you and Jesus. The Lover's whispers begin . . . He calls to you.

the talk

It is when we notice the dirt, that God is most present in us; it is the very sign of his presence.

C. S. LEWIS

Can we follow the savior far, who have no wound or scar?

AMY CARMICHAEL

Let my heart be broken with the things that break God's heart.

BOB PIERCE

What we need to envision falling on us from the sky is God's nourishment, that's all.

SUE MONK KIDD

the word

I was sound asleep, but in my dreams I was wide awake. Oh, listen! It's the sound of my lover knocking, calling!

Song of Songs 5:2 MSG

The LORD spoke to Moses face to face, as a man speaks to his friend.

Exodus 33:11 NKJV

Enoch walked with God; one day Enoch could not be found, because God took him.

Genesis 5:24 NCV

Those who go to God Most High for safety will be protected by the Almighty.

Psalm 91:1 NCV

My soul waits for the Lord more than those who watch for the morning—yes, more than those who watch for the morning.

Psalm 130:6 NKJV

The LORD passed by, and a great and strong wind tore into the mountains and broke the rocks in pieces before the LORD, but the LORD was not in the wind; and after the wind an earthquake . . . and after the earthquake a fire . . . and after the fire a still small voice.

1 Kings 19:11–12 NKJV

Simeon . . . was just and devout, waiting for the Consolation of Israel, and the Holy Spirit was upon him . . . Anna, a prophetess . . . was a widow of about eighty-four years, who did not depart from the temple, but served God with fastings and prayers night and day.

Luke 2:25, 36–37 NKJV

Intimacy

the intimacy tools

Read it . . .

Abba's Child
Brennan Manning
The cry of the heart for intimate belonging.

The Dangerous Duty of Delight
John Piper
Glorifying God, satisfying your soul.

The Jesus I Never Knew
Philip Yancey
Unwrapping the humanity of Jesus.

Jesus the One and Only
Beth Moore
He is all you need!

The Journey of Desire
John Eldredge
Tapping God's imprint on your heart.

Just Give Me Jesus
Anne Graham Lotz
Drawing close to Jesus in all your questions.

Soul Space
Jerome Daley
Finding intimacy with God in a busy world.

The Practice of the Presence of God
Brother Andrew
A timeless classic.

Surf it . . .

www.grahamcooke.com
Resources and events from Graham Cooke.

www.justsmile.ipbhost.com
Forum for teens.

www.liveinhispresence.com
Articles and products related to pursuing Jesus.

Hear it . . .

Casting Crowns, Casting Crowns

Devotion, Newsboys

Friendship and the Fear, Matt Redman

Hungry, Vineyard

Stay, Jeremy Camp

Undone, Mercy Me

When Deep Calls to Deep, Paul Oakley

Do it . . .

Free spiritual retreats in Florida for those in ministry,
www.beside-stillwaters.org.

Retreats for spiritual renewal,
www.brennanmanning.com.

TOP TEN

The Top Ten Ways to Draw Close to God

10 Each morning when you wake up, start thanking God for a new day.

9 Sing or say words that tell God how big and beautiful He is.

8 Take one whole day to just be with God—journal, pray, listen.

7 Read books that draw you closer to God and enlarge your view of Him.

6 Practice sitting quietly with your mind clear, free of thoughts, to listen.

5 Memorize a new verse each week from God's own writings.

4 Pray the Bible—let its truths examine you and lead you to the Truth.

3 Carry on conversations with God throughout the day.

2 Let Jesus carry your heavy thoughts, complex issues, and unsolvable problems.

1 Learn God's love language called "pursuit."

The Question

Are you confident that intimacy with Jesus can satisfy you more than any other relationship?

Any Christ-follower would know to answer this question in the affirmative. But what your head believes is not always what your heart believes. Right? If Christians were convinced of this truth throughout their entire beings, wouldn't their lives reflect this in notable ways?

It is sometimes said that your life shows what you believe in the deepest part of yourself. Let's get real. Sometimes a relationship with a pint of Häagen-Dazs ice cream feels more satisfying than reading God's Word. Sometimes it's the sports section or a shopping trip that feeds your soul more than prayer. When it comes to intimacy with God, why does your heart sometimes lack conviction?

For many reasons. Volume, tangibility, impatience, among others.

For some reason, your lesser appetites—for food, sleep, or entertainment—yell a lot louder than your spiritual appetites. It's just a fact. But the New Rebellion generation learns how to turn down the volume on lesser appetites and turn up the volume on the appetite for intimacy.

> The spiritual rebel tunes his or her soul to recognize and pursue the intangible rewards of intimacy.

And then there's the tangibility factor that draws you to your five natural senses more strongly than you are drawn to the intangible matters of the soul. But long after a craving for ice cream passes, your soul will hunger for the closeness of your heavenly Lover and be satisfied with His gentle presence in your heart. The spiritual rebel tunes his or her soul to recognize and pursue the intangible rewards of intimacy.

Finally, since intimacy is relational, it takes time—and patience—to cultivate. There is no drive-through line for intimacy, which means that those with less passion than you will give up during the waiting times and run on to lesser things. But the soul knows no substitute for real intimacy. Don't be fooled by the counterfeits.

Whenever we move into a new spiritual dimension of our calling and our ministry, we must take the time to upgrade our relationship with God.
Graham Cooke

Friend of God

GRAHAM COOKE
A Prophetic Voice
from England

In Psalm 46:10, God told David, "Be still, and know that I am God." It was a word that brought a profound sense of the presence of God to David in what were difficult circumstances. It's interesting that Psalm 46 began with an earthquake and finished with "Be still." Only God can talk about stillness in the midst of an earthquake.

Graham Cooke

Once in a while a man or woman comes along with both an exceptional life and an exceptional ability to convey that life to others. When it comes to intimacy with God, Graham Cooke is such a person. Originally part of a network of churches in England, Graham now lives and bases his ministry in Vacaville, California. From there, he speaks across the country, helping to build individuals and churches who are both grounded in the character of God and equipped to pursue their supernatural destiny in God.

Intimacy utilizes many skills of the soul. Graham commented on using the skill of stillness in your pursuit of God:

"Being still opens a channel of communication between us and Heaven. All of us have a background conversation going on in our minds. Head noise . . . is an internal voice, a soundtrack for our lives . . . an ongoing, one-way, stream of consciousness conversation, commenting on our lives as it unfolds. Stillness is not about getting somewhere quiet, although that often helps, but about stilling that voice in your head . . . And you can do it, because God is in you."

Several years ago, Graham found himself in a situation that required this kind of stillness. His friend had a brain tumor that had grown to the size of a tennis ball. In a prayer meeting of two hundred people, confusion reigned, but Graham picked out thirty-five of them in quiet faith, and they met alone the following night. After worshiping for some time, he handed each a piece of paper and told them to get still before God and listen.

Coming back together, they compared notes and found that God had spoken clearly and consistently. Now they were able to pray in unity! Going in for surgery, the man asked for one final CAT scan—the tumor was gone. This is the power of intimacy.

Are you tired? Worn out? Burned out on religion? Come to me. Get away with me and you'll recover your life . . . Walk with me and work with me—watch how I do it. Learn the unforced rhythms of grace . . . Keep company with me and you'll learn to live freely and lightly.
Matthew 11:28–30 MSG

wisdom from the now

Don't ask yourself what the world needs. Ask yourself what makes you come alive, and go do that, because what the world needs is people who have come alive.

Gil Bailie

Coming Fully Alive

People spend most of their lives trying to obtain the things they crave, pretending to be somebody else, and being afraid of who they are. Fear, greed, and pride join forces to attack the very identity and ability of every man and woman. And shame is the weapon.

Against this host of enemies, God's Word speaks brilliantly and forcefully: "I knew you before I formed you in your mother's womb. Before you were born I set you apart and appointed you as my spokesman to the world" (Jeremiah 1:5 NLT). Into every heart, God wisely assembled a set of gifts and talents uniquely designed to fulfill one specific destiny. Implicit in this action is a charge to you: Know who you are and use what He has given you to speak to the world.

Gifts & Talents

1 the buzz

In just the last couple of decades, a host of resources have been released to help you better understand your soul. Personality profiles, motivational gifts, love languages, learning styles, vocational evaluations—all these are tools to help you better understand who God has made you to be and what His destiny is for your life.

But while your present abilities and their future use are related, it is important to understand that they are not the same thing. Identifying your gifts and talents is like learning which golf clubs are in your bag. Understanding your gifts is like going to the driving range and practicing with the various woods and irons. Then those talents and abilities have to be placed into the context of what's ahead for you, into God's custom-crafted call to change your world.

I remind you to stir up the gift of God which is in you through the laying on of my hands.
2 Timothy 1:6 NKJV

God is the One who packed your golf bag and determined who you are. God alone knows your future and has empowered you to fulfill your calling by using your unique gifts. But as long as they stay in the bag, they are impotent and their Kingdom purpose is denied. It is in the act of taking hold of your abilities, trusting your Creator, and then partnering with Him to release those gifts that God is honored and His plans fulfilled.

Too many gifted Christians spend their abilities in honest pursuits but fall far short of their calling. Why is that? The expectations and pressures of other people. The desire for material and social success. Trying to follow in someone else's footsteps and imitate another's destiny. Perhaps the largest reason of all is simply the *lack of courage* to follow your heart. Whatever the cause, there are few things more tragic than leading a "normal life."

Graham Cooke said, "God has not called us to do what seems possible, reasonable, or normally attainable . . . We're supposed to be doing what is impossible and outrageous." If that is true, then it's not enough to know your gifts and abilities. That is an important beginning, but then Jesus wants to take you by the hand and lead you out onto the fairway of His choosing, tee up a ball, and hand you a club from your bag.

> God alone knows your future and has empowered you to fulfill your calling by using your unique gifts.

There are many forces that make up who you are—personality, gender, and history, as well as your spiritual and natural giftings. It's up to God to select those forces and call them toward purpose. It's up to you to understand them and release them toward that purpose. Your calling is to take those raw talents—intelligence, artistic ability, athletic strength, relational skills, interests and passions—and cultivate them through learning and practice.

Gifts & Talents

the insight

Acts 6:1–7 marks an epiphany in the life of the disciples and the emergent church. The original twelve disciples found themselves in the midst of an extraordinary and exciting chaos as the new church was exploding into life all around them. The outpouring of God's Spirit at Pentecost, miracles breaking out all around, thousands coming to faith—it was all a broiling mass of wonderful confusion.

> Who you are needs to define what you do in life. Your gifts—your God-given design—will lead you toward your purpose.

As a result, the Twelve found themselves in the same position many entrepreneurs experience in a rapidly growing company: Their original expertise and creative spark became engulfed in management issues. Instead of continuing to chart a course forward, they became professional firefighters, trying to solve a host of emerging problems.

The real danger in all this—and the potential danger in your life—is that the circumstances of your life begin to define who you are. Instead, who you are needs to define what you do in life. Your gifts—your God-given design—will lead you toward your purpose.

In an *aha!* moment, the twelve disciples realized that their ministry and calling had been commandeered by administrative matters, in this case distributing food to the hungry and needy within their community. It's not that this part of the church ministry was "beneath" them; it's just that they had begun to operate outside of their gifts and calling. And when you do that for long, the grace of God begins to fade. The joy fades. The work becomes laborious and frustrating. These symptoms are clues that you might be moving outside your God-given design.

So one day, the Twelve suddenly had a revelation: "Wait a minute! This isn't who we are. We're not administrators; our calling is prayer and preaching. We've really gotten outside our gifting." Of course, they couldn't have even had this awakening if they didn't know who they were and who they weren't. They then moved to identify other leaders who *were* gifted administratively. Brilliant!

There are times in life where you have to do certain things just because they are obligations, not because you're gifted. That is a reality. But it is important to know when you have a choice, and then shift toward activities that are a true expression of your calling in both career and ministry. You reach for the opportunities that are consistent with your gifts. Just as the disciples did.

Gifts & Talents

the point

God didn't make you generic. God is a specialist, and His design on your life is highly specialized. That's why He used the imagery of a physical body in 1 Corinthians 12—the "body" of Christ needs each individual, specialized part in order to function correctly. Knowing God intimately will release you to know yourself intimately . . . so that you can partner with Him in your destiny.

the talk

There is nothing with which every [person] is so afraid as getting to know how enormously much [they] are capable of doing and becoming.

SØREN KIERKEGAARD

Our greatest personal strengths when pushed out of balance become our greatest weaknesses.

GARY SMALLEY

We all need to ditch our captivity to "what will people think?"

ANONYMOUS

Our talents are the gift that God gives to us. What we make of our talents is our gift back to God.

LEO BUSCAGLIA

the word

You should seek after love, and you should truly want to have the spiritual gifts, especially the gift of prophecy.

1 Corinthians 14:1 NCV

Each person is given something to do that shows who God is: Everyone gets in on it, everyone benefits. All kinds of things are handed out by the Spirit, and to all kinds of people! The variety is wonderful.

1 Corinthians 12:7–8 MSG

We were all baptized into one body through one Spirit. And we were all made to share in the one Spirit. The human body has many parts . . . Truly God put all the parts, each one of them, in the body as he wanted them . . . The eye cannot say to the hand, "I don't need you!" And the head cannot say to the foot, "I don't need you!"

1 Corinthians 12:13–14, 19–21 NCV

It is the same with you. Since you want spiritual gifts very much, seek most of all to have the gifts that help the church grow stronger.

1 Corinthians 14:12 NCV

Above all things have fervent love for one another, for "love will cover a multitude of sins." Be hospitable to one another without grumbling. As each one has received a gift, minister it to one another, as good stewards of the manifold grace of God. If anyone speaks, let him speak as the oracles of God. If anyone ministers, let him do it as with the ability which God supplies, that in all things God may be glorified through Jesus Christ.

1 Peter 4:8–11 NKJV

Gifts & Talents

the gifts & talents tools

Read it . . .

All About Talent: Discovering your Gifts and Personality
Larry Burkett
Understanding yourself and how God intends for you to flourish.

Find Your Fit
Kevin Johnson
Manual for teens with stories and personality tests.

The Five Love Languages
Gary Chapman
Learn how to give and receive love effectively.

Leading Talents, Leading Teams: Aligning People, Passions, and Positions for Maximum Performance
Lee Ellis
Creating synergy among people's abilities.

Secret Power for Girls: Identity, Security, and Self-Respect in Troubling Times
Susie Shellenberger
Unlocking the female heart.

Uprising: A Revolution of the Soul
Erwin Raphael McManus
A personal guide for a soul unleashing.

Surf it . . .

www.actsalive.com
Online community to activate your gifts for God.

www.autobahn.mb.ca/~claireh/ambassador.html
Resource for Christian arts.

www.theseeker.org/gifts
Comprehensive study of spiritual gifts.

Hear it . . .

Dichotomy, Grits

Everyday People, Nicole C. Mullen

The Miseducation of Lauryn Hill, Lauryn Hill

No Name Face, Lifehouse

Psalms, Hymns and Spiritual Songs, Donnie McClurkin

Woven and Spun, Nicole Nordman

Do it . . .

Bible study on spiritual gifts, www.christianity.com.

Spiritual gifts analysis, www.church-growth.org/cgi-cg/gifts.cgi.

Another Bible study, www.keyway.ca/htm2002/spirtgif.htm.

TOP TEN

The Top Ten Ways to Activate Your Gifts

10 Consider classes or seminars to develop your natural gifts.

9 Take a spiritual gifts evaluation (see Do it . . . on page 78).

8 Ask your friends and close family what gifts they see in you.

7 Tell God you "eagerly desire spiritual gifts" (1 Corinthians 14:1 NIV), and see what He does.

6 Talk to your pastor about outlets for your gifts.

5 Experiment with your spiritual gifts in your small group.

4 Spend time with someone who is spiritually mature in the areas of your giftings.

3 Read a book on spiritual gifts.

2 Go to conferences and learn more about gifts.

1 Look for ways to use spiritual gifts in your workplace.

The Question

- →

Do you compare your abilities with other people's and doubt God's choice?

If there is one thing that characterizes the human condition, it's a tendency to self-analyze and self-criticize. The sinful nature inherited from Adam and Eve shows itself in three root issues: fear, pride, and greed. All other sins flow out of these, and the common denominator is a preoccupation with self.

You *fear* situations and people that feel threatening to your well-being. You try to elevate yourself in *pride*, hoping to compensate for what is lacking. And you grasp *greedily* after status and possessions that assign worth and bring pleasure. It's not a pretty picture, and not the way people want to see themselves. But this is what Jesus has saved you from . . . and continues to save you from!

So when you find yourself in the very human place of comparing yourself to others, this is an invitation to humility, faith, and love—which are God's solution to the sinful nature. These are the root virtues that form the foundation of His Kingdom, His character, and His salvation. So first, *humble* yourself to realize you don't need spectacular abilities to be significant in God's world. You don't need any certain talent to obey God . . . just a willing heart.

Second, *trust* God enough to believe that He has already deposited inside you every gift and ability you need. You are not giftless! If you can look with a noncritical eye, you will begin to see and value the unique resources He has lovingly placed inside your soul. You can be confident that you are exactly who you need to be. Cultivate and strengthen those gifts so you can flow in them easily and securely.

> You don't need spectacular abilities to be significant in God's world. You don't need any certain talent to obey God . . . just a willing heart.

Then, choose a life of *love* instead of fear! This is the great crossroads of life, and many unwittingly choose fear. But as John reminds us, "Where God's love is, there is no fear, because God's perfect love drives out fear" (1 John 4:18 NCV).

Those who love to be feared fear to be loved, and they themselves are more afraid than anyone, for whereas other men fear only them, they fear everyone.
Saint Francis de Sales

Breathe on Me Now

KATHRYN SCOTT
Songwriter and Worship Leader

When I was growing up, my Mum was always writing songs. She was the one who made it "normal" to write a song about just about anything . . . and that was the very thing that got me started on this whole journey. I can't thank her enough for being true to who God made her, and sharing that with me.

Kathryn Scott

As a popular songwriter and worship leader in the Vineyard movement, Kathryn began her quest to know herself in the place where every man or woman should begin—in the quest for God. It is apropos that her most well-loved song is entitled "Hungry," because it has been spiritual hunger that has formed the riverbanks of her life, channeling her destiny into the service of God and God's people.

Growing up in her native Ireland, Kathryn formed an early passion for both God and music. Her parents traveled full-time with an evangelist; her dad recorded radio programs while her mum wrote songs and sang. Into this good soil, the seeds of talent were planted—a love for singing and playing the piano. And those skills became an emergent voice for her love for God.

Kathryn and her husband, Alan, now pastor a five-year-old church plant in Portstewart on the north coast of Northern Ireland. Having met a decade ago in Scotland, the two lead Causeway Coast Vineyard Church and juggle the many challenges and rewards of life. Kathryn is mother to two young children, spends two days a week in songwriting, serves the church, and periodically records albums.

"When it comes to recording, or going to lead worship somewhere else, I always check to see if it is the right thing for our family first, and then for our church. If it is, and I think the Lord is opening a door that He wants me to go through, I take it on. If it doesn't match up, then I don't. You don't always get to do everything you would like to, but it does mean that hopefully you only take on the things the Lord wants you to do." By being faithful to the gifts and talents planted inside her, Kathryn has found a rich destiny.

vital stats

- Decision for Jesus: age 3

- First original song: age 9

- Key musical influences: Matt Redman, Brenton Brown, and mentor Brian Doerksen

- Thing she never wanted to do: lead worship

- Current home: Portstewart, Northern Ireland

wisdom from the now

83

Do we have any inner resources at the moment when we are accosted by the Holy One . . . ? Immediately our credentials of independence vanish, and we cease to carry ourselves with the swagger of the executive who knows what's up and has all under control; we become aware of innate poverty, our next-breath dependence, and a numbness that invades the roots of our littleness and realness.

Brennan Manning

Relinquishing the Power Position

There are few things that the human heart craves more than control.

It's the result of our fallen condition, an instinctive yearning to massage the circumstances of life and order the natural world. It's stronger in some than in others, depending upon temperament, but essentially it's the human condition. The expression of "my kingdom come, my will be done."

But Jesus demonstrated a life that was 180 degrees opposite from that. It was perhaps the most extraordinary thing about Jesus: He was the first person ever on planet Earth to surrender His will fully, and delightfully, to Another. That counterintuitive decision paradoxically released Jesus from the slavery of self-will into the heavenly freedom of God-will. So, what does Jesus, in turn, ask of you? Nothing other. And nothing less.

Surrender

the buzz

History is primarily a record of the will of men and women—what people have wanted and what people have obtained, measured in terms of power. You may have never considered yourself hungry for power. You may not even be conscious of how your will expresses itself or tries to shape the people and circumstances around you.

Try this simple exercise: Is it hard for you when the car in front of you won't turn into traffic, even when there's plenty of space for it to pull out? Do you find yourself angry or cynical when God doesn't answer your prayers when and how you want? Or how about this one: Would your friends ever consider you compulsive about cleaning or organizing or talking or reading the news or (fill in the blank)?

Those who try to hold on to their lives will give up true life. Those who give up their lives for me will hold on to true life.

Matthew 10:39 NCV

Without being crippled by it, most people feel driven in some arena of their lives. Driven to sleep, driven to eat, driven to work. Even when a person is labeled as a workaholic, there is usually an underlying admiration being expressed. People's drive to be productive almost always brings great reward and affirmation. But whether society rewards it or rejects it, drivenness is usually an expression of the soul's desire for power and control. And it usually finds itself opposed by God, who retains power and control for Himself.

The solution? Submission.

Submission begins with recognizing what people and circumstances lie within your responsibility. If you are a parent, then you are responsible for your family; if you are an employer, you have responsibility for those who work for you. But outside your relatively small domain, you must resist the urge to push and pull people into what you think is right.

Second, submission looks like obedience, both to God and to the authorities in your life. When you accept the direction that comes from those authorities, then you are obeying God.

> **W**hether society rewards it or rejects it, drivenness is usually an expression of the soul's desire for power and control.
>
>

Third, submission to proper authorities also requires you to resist wrongful authorities, namely, the devil (see James 4:7). God makes it clear that He will share control with no other being, natural or spiritual. Yet in characteristic brilliance, God has granted to you a measure of power, a measure of freedom frequently referred to as *free will*.

The power of choice is a potent freedom, and the consequences of your choices are the difference between heaven or hell influencing earth. Let your heart embrace His goodwill in your life. It's not passivity and it's not fatalism. It's trust and obedience. It's letting God be God. That is the heartbeat of the New Rebellion.

Surrender

the insight

There is a remarkable life-expression of the quality of surrender in the story of Ruth (see the book of Ruth). This ancient woman is a window into God's mind when He envisioned the virtue of surrender. Let's peer through that window . . .

Ruth lived in the country of Moab, probably during the thirteenth century BC. Though Moab was historically an enemy of Israel, Ruth married the son of an Israelite couple who were living in Moab due to famine in their homeland. After Ruth's husband died, her mother-in-law, Naomi, decided to return to her home in Bethlehem, but she urged Ruth to remain in her own land where she was known and where she would have the greatest opportunity for remarrying.

> Surrender voluntarily releases control and trustingly submits in obedience.

Heedless of those words, Ruth begged Naomi to let her go with her. "Don't beg me to leave you or to stop following you. Where you go, I will go. Where you live, I will live. Your people will be my people, and your God will be my God" (Ruth 1:16 NCV).

This was a remarkable loyalty, since Ruth would be a foreigner in Israel, with her only reward being the responsibility of supporting her mother-in-law. When all natural reason shouted for Ruth to remain, she rebelled against the "normal" to surrender her life to an unknown future. That must have required enormous courage, but it opened up a marvelous destiny.

Three notable qualities characterized Ruth's surrender and will characterize yours: Her decision was anchored in relationship, expressed in obedience, and rewarded with unexpected abundance. Ruth's affection for and commitment to her mother-in-law were expansive. The depth of relationship between those women (often unusual in in-law relationships) was the motivating force behind Ruth's surrender.

And it really was a surrender. In that new life, she was utterly powerless and completely dependent upon God. In spite of that risk, Ruth chose to obey Naomi in everything—which became the crucial factor to Ruth's meeting and finding favor with the man who would eventually marry her. Surrender voluntarily releases control and trustingly submits in obedience.

That obedience was then rewarded with unexpected abundance. The favor of God shone on Ruth's surrendered heart, and she became the wife of a wealthy man, the object of his deep affection, and the mother of a new baby boy.

Surrender

the point

Surrender to God not only releases one's own destiny but also releases the larger purposes of God in the world. Ruth's little boy became the forefather of King David and eventually the forefather of Jesus Himself. God never forces you to surrender; He calls you to surrender, motivates you toward surrender, but it must be voluntary. That choice— to lay aside your futile attempts to control life in exchange for His wise, loving rule—will propel you into your future as a world-changer!

the talk

God plays a game with the soul called "the loser wins"; a game in which the one who holds the poorest cards does best. The Pharisee's consciousness that he had such an excellent hand really prevented him from taking a single trick.

EVELYN UNDERHILL

When we know love matters more than anything, and we know that nothing else *really* matters, we move into the state of surrender. Surrender does not diminish our power; it enhances it.

SARA PADDISON

He is no fool who gives what he cannot keep to gain what he cannot lose.

JIM ELLIOT

The true gospel is a call to self-sacrifice not self-fulfillment.

JOHN MACARTHUR

the word

Then Jesus, looking at him, loved him, and said to him, "One thing you lack: Go your way, sell whatever you have and give to the poor, and you will have treasure in heaven; and come, take up the cross, and follow Me."

Mark 10:21 NKJV

You, brethren, have been called to liberty; only do not use liberty as an opportunity for the flesh, but through love serve one another.

Galatians 5:13 NKJV

Suppose a king is about to go to war against another king. Will he not first sit down and consider whether he is able with ten thousand men to oppose the one coming against him with twenty thousand? If he is not able, he will send a delegation while the other is still a long way off and will ask for terms of peace. In the same way, any of you who does not give up everything he has cannot be my disciple.

Luke 14:31–33 NIV

Whoever wants to be great must become a servant. Whoever wants to be first among you must be your slave. That is what the Son of Man has done: He came to serve, not be served—and then to give away his life in exchange for the many who are held hostage.

Matthew 20:27–28 MSG

He took with Him Peter and the two sons of Zebedee, and He began to be sorrowful and deeply distressed. Then He said to them, "My soul is exceedingly sorrowful, even to death. Stay here and watch with Me." He went a little farther and fell on His face, and prayed, saying, "O My Father, if it is possible, let this cup pass from Me; nevertheless, not as I will, but as You will."

Matthew 26:37–39 NKJV

Surrender

the surrender tools

Read it . . .

Absolute Surrender
Andrew Murray
The "blessing condition" of a victorious life.

Celebration of Discipline
Richard Foster
A modern classic of spiritual tools for surrender.

Discipline: The Glad Surrender
Elisabeth Elliot
Ordering your mind, body, possessions, time, and feelings.

The Discipline of Surrender
Douglas Webster
Biblical images of discipleship.

A Hunger for God
John Piper
The rewards from the surrender of fasting.

A Journey in Humility
Steve Harper
The source of surrender is humility.

Let Go
François Fénelon
A series of letters from a seventeenth-century spiritual adviser.

Surf it . . .

www.bible.com/answers/ahumilty.html
Study on humility.

www.suffering.net
A wealth of resources for when surrender hurts.

www.holymyrrhbearers.com/ obedience_beyond_basics.htm
A monastic perspective on obedience.

Hear it . . .

Carry Away, Shane and Shane
Facedown, Matt Redman
For All You've Done, Hillsong
God, Rebecca St. James
Walk On, 4Him
Worship Again, Michael W. Smith

Do it . . .

Go on a short-term missions trip, www.adventures.org.

Opportunities to "adopt" a disadvantaged child, www.children.org.

Surrender to caring: foster care and food relief, www.ne.hopeww.org.

The Top Ten Ways to Relinquish Control

10 Make frequent use of Jesus' prayer, "Not My will, but Yours."

9 Meditate on Jesus' attitude in Philippians 2:1–18, being a servant, humble and obedient.

8 Read Roy Hession's *The Calvary Road* for a new perspective on brokenness and surrender.

7 Make a habit of not making important decisions alone.

6 Live by a schedule that allows for spontaneity and reflection.

5 Experiment with fasting one day a week for a month.

4 Make a list of potential addictions in your life.

3 Ask your best friend if you have any controlling habits.

2 Commit yourself to not motivate people through guilt.

1 This month give away both some money and some time.

The Question

Have you set any-thing in your life off-limits to God?

Sometimes you find yourself in a relationship where a friend has set emotional boundaries, and you are unable to go into certain areas of his or her life. In a close relationship, those sorts of boundaries get in the way of true intimacy and force the connection into more superficial channels. That kind of inequity in capacity or expectation tends to bring disappointment.

Your relationship with God calls for the greatest measure of openness on your part. If you want to be truly intimate with God, delighting in Him and He in you, then transparent self-surrender is a prerequisite. You must be willing to have every part of your life totally given over to God's control. The choice—conscious or not—to compartmentalize certain segments of your life away from God's wise and gentle direction is a mistake. And it will hinder your destiny.

Total abandonment requires total trust. If you trust your heavenly Father more than you trust your senses, then surrender will come easily and naturally. What you see, feel, hear, taste, and smell does convey information but cannot always be trusted completely. People rarely, if ever, want to have something taken away from them. Yet periodically, God knows that the good is the enemy of the best—and takes it. Can you surrender to that expression of His love?

> **I**f you want to be truly intimate with God, delighting in Him and He in you, then transparent self-surrender is a prerequisite.

Jean-Pierre de Caussade said, "With God, the more we seem to lose, the more we gain. The more he takes materially, the more he gives spiritually. We love him partly for his gifts. If they are no longer visible, we come to love him for himself alone." God has so much to give you, and sometimes you don't know how good the gift really is because you are expecting something more known or tangible. Yield to Him, and the rewards of surrender will be yours.

Trust in the LORD with all your heart, and lean not on your own understanding; in all your ways acknowledge Him, and He shall direct your paths. Do not be wise in your own eyes.
Proverbs 3:5–7 NKJV

Surrendered to Her Destiny

HARRIET TUBMAN

1820–1913

Harriet Tubman had been their "Moses" . . . She had faithfully gone down into Egypt, and had delivered these six bondmen by her own heroism. Harriet was a woman of no pretensions . . . Yet, in point of courage, shrewdness and disinterested exertions to rescue her fellow-men, by making personal visits to Maryland among the slaves, she was without her equal.

William Still
From *Fleeing for Freedom: Stories of the Underground Railroad*

Harriet Tubman may be the most ordinary extraordinary person you've ever heard of. Born into slavery in Dorchester County, Maryland, she grew up in an extremely harsh environment. She was denied any formal education and was described as an "ordinary specimen of humanity." Beyond that, at the age of twelve she was severely injured by a blow to the head from an angry slaveowner for refusing to help tie up a runaway; that injury brought about a lifelong ailment of narcolepsy and even sudden blackouts.

This was a woman with every circumstance of life against her and almost none in her favor. Yet she was a woman of faith, and that was enough. Letters about Harriet describe her "highly spiritual nature" as well as her enduring "confidence that God would aid her efforts." And her efforts were such that absolutely required the intervention of God.

Which efforts? After Harriet escaped from slavery herself, she spent the next decade conducting nineteen daring raids back into Maryland to free more slaves—approximately three hundred slaves—along the Underground Railroad into Canada. When the Civil War broke out, she served as a cook, a nurse, a soldier, and a spy. Talk about an extraordinary life of purpose, of calling, and of surrender.!

The godly quality of surrender is framed by the ability to know *whom* to surrender to. Surrender is not, indiscriminately, a virtue; there are many unworthy people who are delighted to accept the allegiance of another's heart. But the New Rebellion calls men and women to a penetrating discernment that illuminates where to rebel and where to submit. Harriet did not surrender to her captors, but having endured the oppressive injustice of slavery, she surrendered instead to her calling and her Lord. The courage and perseverance that prompted this surrender then propelled her into her destiny, a destiny that had an impact on a nation.

wisdom from the past

Money will buy a bed but not sleep, books but not brains, food but not appetite, finery but not beauty, medicine but not health, luxury but not culture, amusement but not happiness, a crucifix but not a Savior, a temple of religion but not heaven.

Anonymous

Who Owns Whom?

Money. Everyone needs it. Everyone wants it. Most people want more than they need. Lots of people need more than they have. Is there anything that so easily becomes the focal point of the human heart?

Among Christians, money is both idolized and vilified. Some segments of the church renounce money for a life of voluntary poverty, citing the example of Christ. Other segments see financial prosperity as indicative of the Kingdom of heaven coming to earth. Some segments of the church collect their weekly tithes and offerings but ignore financial issues from the pulpit.

In short, money makes a great servant but a poor master. Your calling is to use your money, whether little or much, to rebel against the world's system and serve the cause of Christ in the earth.

Money

the buzz

Money was not a subject that Jesus shied away from. But it can be rightly understood only within the context of Jesus' primary message: The Kingdom of God is coming! In the Kingdom economy, money is not the centerpiece as it is in earthly economies; relationships are the currency of God's world. God's heart focuses on people, not possessions. But neither is money irrelevant; it is, in fact, a very powerful force on the earth.

Consider two prime examples: the "rich young ruler" (Mark 10:17–23) and the "good Samaritan" (Luke 10:30–37). Both of those men were wealthy, but one found his money to be an obstacle to Kingdom purposes while the other used his money to advance God's purposes. And this was the crux of the matter: the heart.

The first man was sincere, humble, and motivated to please God. His honest inquiries of how to obtain eternal life endeared him to Jesus; the passage says Jesus looked at him and loved him. But Jesus also knew that money had become the place of security and comfort for this fellow, that this dynamic would render him impotent in the Kingdom. So to set this man free from his addiction, Jesus told him that the money would have to go. It was a hindrance to his pursuit of God; it

No one can serve two masters. The person will hate one master and love the other, or will follow one master and refuse to follow the other. You cannot serve both God and worldly riches.

Matthew 6:24 NCV

was, in fact, his god. Unfortunately, the roots of that entanglement were too deep, and he would not turn it loose.

The Samaritan, on the other hand, was completely free with the wealth entrusted to him. Rather than being the object of misplaced loyalty, money was his servant to further the interests of God. And this becomes evident as the story unfolds and shows him using that money to heal and restore a wounded traveler from a country hostile to him.

> **W**here you spend your money shows very accurately what is truly important to you. Are these things also important to God?

This is the same challenge you face today: Is money your servant or master? So how do you know which it is? Probably the easiest way to know the place money has in your heart is to take a blood pressure reading when you suddenly have a great sum added or taken away. Does your attitude change? Does your faith change? Are you a different person as a result?

Another challenge: Flip through your checkbook register and ponder your spending habits. Where you spend your money shows very accurately what is truly important to you. Are these things also important to God? How many expenditures are irrelevant to the Kingdom; how many reinforce His values? This is the way God's new rebels think!

Money

the insight

If you read through all the passages in God's Word that discuss the topic of money, you will find quite a spectrum of perspectives, even places that appear to speak to opposite sides of the issue. The book of Proverbs consistently treats wealth as an evidence of God's blessing and offers wise counsel for obtaining it, guarding it, and increasing it.

> Many profound truths from God seem to be found—and understood accurately—only within a tension, somehow suspended between two competing ideas.

The Sermon on the Mount, in contrast, finds Jesus teaching the disciples to not store up treasures on earth or to worry about food or clothing for tomorrow. Instead, they are to pursue the interests of the Kingdom of God and trust Him to provide for their natural needs. So which is it?

Many profound truths from God seem to be found—and understood accurately—only within a *tension*, somehow suspended between two competing ideas. For example, the prevailing will of God and the free will of men and women. So when it comes to money, there appear to be both valid and invalid uses for wealth. And as in many things, it hinges upon a heart condition.

But the trouble lies in the heart: The heart is cleverly adept at deceiving itself. This means that frequently we don't know our own motivations. To counter this new tension, here are six biblical benchmarks to regularly measure your heart against:

1. Priority: If the values and purposes of God are foremost in your affections, then money will find its correct place in your thinking (see Matthew 6:19–24).

2. Dependency: If your security lies in God and not in possessions, then He can trust you to use possessions without undue attachment (see Matthew 6:25–34).

3. Generosity: If you are consistently prepared to use your finances to honor God and bless others, then He will increase your supply (see 1 Corinthians 9:5–15).

4. Contentment: If your joy and confidence remain equally strong during times of lavish abundance and times of painful lack, you will be empowered toward your God-given destiny (see Philippians 4:11–13).

5. Stewardship: If you are faithful with your resources and use them to provide for those entrusted to your care, then God will honor you with greater authority (see Matthew 25:14–29).

6. Freedom: If you avoid the seductive temptation of debt and live within your means, then you will be free to obey God whenever and wherever He directs you (see Proverbs 22:7; Romans 13:7–8).

the point

Paul makes the explicit connection between earthly wealth and heavenly wealth in 1 Timothy 6:17–19. The possessions of this world have a purpose, and that purpose is to enable godly actions in the earth, specifically, the opportunity to share with those in need. When money is used in this way, it becomes mystically transformed into an eternal treasure. The conclusion: Money is a Kingdom resource that transcends the boundary between earth and heaven.

the talk

It is not persecution of the church in China that I fear. The church has always been able to weather persecution. My fear is the love of money in the church.

A CHINESE PASTOR

No one would remember the Good Samaritan if he'd only had good intentions—he had money, too.

MARGARET THATCHER

There are three conversions necessary: the conversion of the heart, mind, and the purse.

MARTIN LUTHER

Prosperity knits a man to the World. He feels that it is "finding his place in it," while really it is finding its place in him.

C. S. LEWIS

the word

"Bring to the storehouse a full tenth of what you earn so there will be food in my house. Test me in this," says the LORD All-Powerful. "I will open the windows of heaven for you and pour out all the blessings you need."

Malachi 3:10 NCV

If you want to give, your gift will be accepted. It will be judged by what you have, not by what you do not have.

2 Corinthians 8:12 NCV

I have been young, and now am old; yet I have not seen the righteous forsaken, nor his descendants begging bread. He is ever merciful, and lends; and his descendants are blessed.

Psalm 37:25–26 NKJV

He who loves silver will not be satisfied with silver; nor he who loves abundance, with increase. This also is vanity.

Ecclesiastes 5:10 NKJV

Some people give much but get back even more. Others don't give what they should and end up poor. Whoever gives to others will get richer; those who help others will themselves be helped.

Proverbs 11:24–25 NCV

I say to GOD, "Be my Lord!" Without you, nothing makes sense . . . My choice is you, GOD, first and only. And now I find I'm *your* choice! You set me up with a house and yard. And then you made me your heir! The wise counsel GOD gives when I'm awake is confirmed by my sleeping heart. Day and night I'll stick with GOD; I've got a good thing going and I'm not letting go. I'm happy from the inside out, and from the outside in, I'm firmly formed.

Psalm 16:2, 5–9 MSG

Money

the money tools

Read it . . .

God and Your Stuff
Wesley K. Willmer & Martyn Smith
The vital link between your possessions
and your soul.

Master Your Money
Ron Blue
A new theory of financial planning from
the Bible.

Money and Possessions
Kay and David Arthur
A six-week study to discover God's view
on wealth.

Money Before Marriage
Larry Burkett
Solving money problems before build-
ing your new life together.

Money, Possessions, and Eternity
Randy Alcorn
Rethinking financial attitudes for eternal
impact.

**Put Your Money Where Your
Morals Are**
Scott Fehrenbacher
Advice for values-based investing.

**Total Money Makeover: A Proven
Plan for Financial Fitness**
Dave Ramsey
An easy plan for "financial fitness."

Surf it . . .

www.acts17-11.com/money.html
Biblical perspectives from the
VanDruffs.

www.financialfoundationbuilders.com
Financial tools for good management.

www.thegoodsteward.com
Articles and resources for Christian
stewardship.

Hear it . . .

The Answer to the Question, Tree 63

Brent Jones and the T.P. Mobb,
Brent Jones

Carried Me: The Worship Project,
Jeremy Camp

Crashings, Falling Up

Famished, Three Strand

Real, The Tommies

Do it . . .

*Devotionals, small group studies,
and academic articles by topic*,
www.virtualbibleschool.com.

*Take a class on managing your
money at an online Bible training
school*, www.crown.org.

TOP TEN

The Top Ten Warnings That You Are Materialistic

10 You subtly resent giving your tithe in church.

9 You need to work overtime just so you can buy the latest fashions.

8 You find it difficult to give generously to your friends or family.

7 You constantly talk and think about money.

6 You secretly want others to admire your possessions.

5 You like to show off your latest "toys."

4 You label people who are poor as lazy and unmotivated.

3 You pride yourself in buying only the best products.

2 You respect wealthy people and value their opinions more than the opinions of others who are less well off.

1 You extend yourself to help others only when it profits you.

The Question

Are you willing to give away a significant amount of what you earn to help those in need?

It is deceptively easy to be assimilated by a world driven by greed. You know that the seen is not as real as the unseen, yet the visible captures your attention with its emotional volume. It's easy to lose your focus and think that you need more and more, not being content with what you have.

The ubiquitous question "What would Jesus do?" could, in this case, be more appropriately replaced with "What *did* Jesus do?" The answer is that Jesus chose for Himself a life of material simplicity. But you also get the impression that He could just as easily have had abundance; the bottom line is that possessions had no hold upon Jesus' heart and mission. And neither should they define yours.

How important is the car you drive, the clothes you wear, the "toys" you have? The simple way to know whether you possess your things or whether they possess you is to imagine not having them. Are they an idol in your life? Well, try it on for size: Would you be devastated if something happened to them, and they were suddenly gone? Take a blood pressure reading.

Freedom from being owned by things ushers you into the radical and enviable position of being able to help others—a big-time Kingdom value and an overarching characteristic of Jesus' ministry. You don't have to travel to a third-world country to readily find those who don't have a home to sleep in or enough food to eat. Are you prepared to give money you have labored for to those whose needs exceed yours? When you can give an honest yes to that question, then your money has become a potent resource for God's Kingdom.

> The simple way to know whether you possess your things or whether they possess you is to imagine not having them.

You are rich if you have had a meal today.
Billy Graham

You Get to Give

DAVE RAMSEY
Hip Financial Guru

You can get anywhere if you simply go one step at a time. God tends to pour blessing on people going in a direction He wants them to go.

Dave Ramsey

Ramsey always had a head for business. By the time he was twenty-six years old, he was worth more than four million dollars through shrewd investments in real estate. But apparently, it wasn't quite shrewd enough, because only four years later Ramsey declared personal bankruptcy when banks started calling in some of his mortgage notes. Dave had leveraged his business too hard and too far.

After losing everything, he had to take a hard look at how this disaster had happened. The insights he acquired led him to start the Lampo Group in 1988 as a counseling resource to help others avoid bankruptcy and foreclosure. He eventually got back into real estate investing, but this time he did it without personal debt. Within a few years, Ramsey was back on his feet and was the host of a nationally syndicated radio program.

The Dave Ramsey Show is heard by more than two million listeners each week on more than 240 radio stations throughout the United States. The three-hour live-radio talk show focuses on life, love, and relationships, and how they happen to revolve around money.

By stressing debt-free investing, Ramsey bucks the usual investment wisdom and steers a course that is both radical and biblical. One of his passions is helping Christians find financial stability, emotional peace, and the freedom to give generously in the Kingdom of God.

Ramsey is totally up front that his advice is just plain common sense. "Broke is normal. Why be normal?" he declares famously. The problem in personal finance, according to Ramsey, is 80 percent behavior and only 20 percent head knowledge: We know what to do, we just don't do it. He's plainspoken, has a good sense of humor, is very practical, and isn't pushy about his Christian faith.

Dave Ramsey's "Baby Steps":

1. Put at least $1,000 in an emergency fund in the bank.

2. Pay off all debt, smallest first.

3. Build your emergency fund to 3–6 months of expenses.

4. Invest 15 percent of household income into pretax retirement accounts.

5. Save for your kids' college.

6. Pay off your home early.

7. Build wealth and give! Invest in mutual funds and real estate.

wisdom from the now

So it is within our spirits (small *s*),
as distinct from our souls, that
the Spirit (big *S*) comes to live.
Our spirits have direct communion
with God's Spirit as we cultivate
the spiritual life.

Jerome Daley

Got Fuel?

When the gas gauge in your car starts banging on *E*, you'd better get motivated to find a gas station; otherwise, you'll soon be stranded. There are lots of stranded Christians—Christians who want to live a spiritually significant life but are not getting their "tanks" filled with the Spirit's power. Are you one?

Spiritual fuel was such a pivotal issue to Jesus that He effectively put the entire birth of the church on hold until that fuel was available. In His closing words before He ascended into heaven, Jesus gave strict instructions to His disciples to do nothing until "clothed with power from on high" (Luke 24:49 NIV). Picture it: Coming on the heels of His exhilarating defeat of death and His electrifying charge to take the good news into the entire earth, Jesus' final word was, "Do nothing. Wait until I deliver fuel to empower you."

God's Spirit

the buzz

This current generation is arguably the most "spiritual" generation in five hundred years. Since the world shifted from its medieval mind-set to a modern, "enlightened" mind-set, people have never so acknowledged the existence of and, increasingly, the importance of the spiritual dimension in the earth.

Paul was at the exact same point two thousand years ago as he declared to the city of Corinth, "My speech and my preaching were not with persuasive words of human wisdom, but in demonstration of the Spirit and of power" (1 Corinthians 2:4 NKJV). What a thing to say! Was Paul running down his ability as a speaker, or was he calling attention to something much more important? Though unflattering, it may not be inaccurate to describe the last five hundred years of the church as an infatuation with "wise and persuasive words" as leaders have targeted the mind rather than the heart.

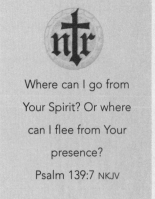

Where can I go from Your Spirit? Or where can I flee from Your presence?

Psalm 139:7 NKJV

Now more than ever, Paul's words ring with clarity and conviction across the spiritual landscape of this world: If you are going to make a Kingdom impact on planet Earth, according to Jesus' commission, it will come only through "a demonstration of" the Spirit's power. It was true at Pentecost, and it is true today: By and large, people don't want information about God, they want God Himself. They want a relational encounter with the spiritual realm. Fortunately, this is what God wants as well.

God has prepared this generation for an unprecedented spiritual awakening by releasing an unprecedented spiritual hunger. It is quite literally a match made in heaven. But it requires God's people to become intimate with God's Spirit as never before—to know Him, His ways, His heartbeat, His passion—and to walk in unparalleled partnership with Him. You can't lead someone where you haven't gone yourself.

And this is how you go there: Cultivate intimacy through focused time. Practice your spiritual gifts. Expect God to move miraculously through you. As you observe

> By and large, people don't want information about God, they want God Himself.

what God is doing, be willing to ask Him for the "big stuff." For healing. For salvation. For whole groups of people to be affected by God. Ask God to back up spiritual words with spiritual power.

The ancient prophets were led by the Spirit (see Ezekiel 37:1). Simeon was led by the Spirit (see Luke 2:27). Jesus was led by the Spirit (see Luke 4:1). Paul was led by the Spirit (see Acts 20:22). Are you led by the Spirit? The Spirit is available to you and wants to guide you into a powerful partnership with Him.

Don't get stranded. Get the fuel.

God's Spirit

the insight

Who better to teach you the purpose and operation of God's Spirit than the One who sent Him?

Jesus found it difficult to convince His disciples that His leaving would truly be better for them than His staying (see John 14). Before experiencing the live-in presence of God's Spirit, it was hard for them to imagine anything better than Jesus being there.

> **W**hen you stay connected to Jesus, God's Spirit flows into your life nonstop.

So Jesus took an extended time to explain how vital this new "fuel" was going to be in their lives. In this intimate time together, He conveyed five irreplaceable functions that the Spirit would play inside them. And those are the roles He will play in your life as well.

First, God's Spirit will be an ever-present representative of God's Kingdom—a personal ambassador of heaven's values and agenda. If you plan to partner with God in His move in the earth, this is like having a red phone: a direct line to the Commanding Officer. You will never be alone, never abandoned or isolated in the battle.

Second, God's Spirit will constantly tutor you in the culture of heaven so that you become more and more a citizen of that Kingdom. He will remind you of Jesus' words, prompting you with biblical truth right when you need it, and also continue to teach you things that you've never heard or seen before. This is a life-coach of the highest order.

Third, the Spirit will provide a constant flow of spiritual vitality to your inner life. This is pictured in the whole image of the vine: God the Father is the gardener, God the Son is the vine, and by implication God the Spirit is the "sap" that brings every essential nutrient to you, the branch. When you stay connected to Jesus, God's Spirit flows into your life nonstop.

Fourth, the Spirit will be an anchor of unchanging truth in the midst of a wave-tossed world that is dying for truth. He will confirm truth to you, and He will also bring a confrontational conviction upon the world. Of course, some will rally to that convicting truth and others will hate it.

Finally, God's Spirit will function as a window of revelation, a portal into Kingdom realities that are not yet pres-ent in this earthly realm. He promises to reveal future events as well as reveal the mind of Jesus to you (see John 16:13–15).

God's Spirit

the point

These are the roles the Spirit wants to take in your life: Heavenly Liaison, Kingdom Adviser, Spiritual Nutritionist, Imposing Bodyguard, and Strategic Planner. It's like having an entire staff at your disposal. If you listen to the Spirit in these various roles, you absolutely cannot lose. He will connect you, correct you, sustain you, protect you, and direct you in everything you do. He is the empowering fuel for all your Kingdom activity.

the talk

The Holy Spirit establishes the righteousness of heaven in the midst of the unrighteousness of earth, and will not stop or stay until all that is dead has been brought back to life and a new world has come into being.

KARL BARTH

The Holy Spirit is a Person. He is not enthusiasm. He is not courage. He is not energy . . . He has individuality. He is one being and not another. He has will and intelligence. He has hearing. He has knowledge and sympathy and ability to love and see and think. He can hear, speak, desire, grieve, and rejoice. He is a Person.

A. W. TOZER

There are thousands of professing Christians who think they have been justified, who think their sins are forgiven, and that they are on their way to heaven, who show no evidence of the regenerating work of the Holy Spirit in their lives.

JERRY BRIDGES

the word

I will pray the Father, and He will give you another Helper, that He may abide with you forever—the Spirit of truth, whom the world cannot receive, because it neither sees Him nor knows Him; but you know Him, for He dwells with you and will be in you.

John 14:16–17 NKJV

You are not ruled by your sinful selves. You are ruled by the Spirit, if that Spirit of God really lives in you. But the person who does not have the Spirit of Christ does not belong to Christ.

Romans 8:9 NCV

God has shown us these things through the Spirit. The Spirit searches out all things, even the deep secrets of God.

1 Corinthians 2:10 NCV

Do not cast me away from Your presence, and do not take Your Holy Spirit from me.

Psalm 51:11 NKJV

Be filled with the Spirit, speaking to one another in psalms and hymns and spiritual songs, singing and making melody in your heart to the Lord, giving thanks always for all things to God the Father in the name of our Lord Jesus Christ, submitting to one another in the fear of God.

Ephesians 5:18–21 NKJV

We're able to stretch our hands out and receive what we asked for because we're doing what he said, doing what pleases him . . . As we keep his commands, we live deeply and surely in him, and he lives in us. And this is how we experience his deep and abiding presence in us: by the Spirit he gave us.

1 John 3:22, 24 MSG

God's Spirit

the God's Spirit tools

Read it . . .

All About the Holy Spirit
Herbert Lockyer
An exploration of every biblical reference.

The Fire That Ignites: Living in the Power of the Holy Spirit
Tony Evans
Wisdom for shaping Spirit-led habits.

The Holy Spirit
Billy Graham
A vivid portrait of the ministry of the Spirit.

The Holy Spirit Unleashed in You
Kay Arthur
Kay's study on the book of Acts.

Hosting the Holy Spirit
Che Ahn
Welcoming and making room for God's Spirit.

The Nature of God
Graham Cooke
Having a closer relationship with God's Spirit.

The Promise of God's Power: Discovering Life in the Holy Spirit
Jim Cymbala
Tapping the power for transformation in your life and church.

Surf it . . .

www.holyspiritinteractive.net
Catholic perspectives on the Spirit.

www.oru.edu/university/library/holy spirit/index.html
Pentecostal database of 15,000+ resources.

www.spirithome.com/spirpers.html
Biblical thoughts on God's Spirit as a person.

Hear it . . .

Acoustic Hymns, Mark Magnuson

Ardent Worship: Skillet Live, Skillet

iWorship: Next, Various Artists

Once Upon a Shattered Life, Seventh Day Slumber

Room to Breathe, ZOEgirl

Satisfy, Kathryn Scott

The Blueprint Dives, Extol

Do it . . .

Try a game, www.bible.ca/trinity/trinity-holy-spirit-game.htm.

Take a spiritual gifts inventory, www.motivationalliving.com/theholy spirit/default.asp.

The Top Ten Indications of the Spirit's Activity in Your Life

10   You find it unexpectedly easier to be patient and kind (see Galatians 5:22).

9   You sense a sudden urgency to pray for a friend or family member.

8   You long to spend time with God and be in His presence.

7   The Bible makes sense to you as never before.

6   Scriptures to encourage others pop into your mind.

5   Your appetite for God's Word gets stronger and stronger.

4   You may develop a unique prayer language just between you and Him.

3   You may have dreams that illuminate God's heart.

2   You sense God's nearness and comfort when you are grieving.

1   You feel an unexplainable peace in the midst of stressful circumstances.

The Question

Is God's Spirit able to move freely in your life, or is the Spirit inhibited because of your fears?

The Spirit of God is a mysterious force in your life, but it should never be an intimidating one. Jesus sent the Spirit to His followers when He went back to heaven. At that time, He assured them, "It is for your good that I am going away. Unless I go away, the Counselor will not come to you; but if I go, I will send him to you" (John 16:7 NIV). The empowering fuel of the Spirit was, and is, one of the most tangible expressions of God's goodness to His people.

Intimidation creeps in when your trust in His goodness is overcome by your instinct to try to control. But that's the thing about the Spirit—He requires you to relinquish your control to Him; otherwise, He will not move. God's people frequently and unintentionally shut down the moving of the Spirit by intuitively reaching to control the situation, whether it's at work or at home or at church. But this is coun-terproductive to the life you were made for.

The Spirit is good and wants to make Himself heard in your life. The prophet Elijah discovered that the Spirit does not usually come in a strong wind, an earthquake, or a fire—not usually in obvious, in-your-face kinds of ways. He is more subtle; He typically comes to you in a gentle whisper. And that whisper can be eas-ily missed when there's too much emotional noise around.

When you learn to quiet your soul to listen, you may be surprised at all that you hear. Wisdom, comfort, peace, truth, encouragement . . . all these things come from God's Spirit to His children. Why would you be fearful of God moving in your life? Open up your spiritual ears and let the gentle whisper speak to you today.

It is through The Word, and the Word Alone, that the Spirit teaches, apply-ing the general prin-ciples or promises to our special need. And it is The Spirit, and the Spirit Alone, who can really make the word a light on our path.
Andrew Murray

The LORD passed by, and a great and strong wind tore into the mountains and broke the rocks in pieces before the LORD, but the LORD was not in the wind; and after the wind an earthquake . . . and after the earthquake a fire . . . and after the fire a still small voice.
1 Kings 19:11–12 NKJV

Surprised by the Power of the Spirit

JACK DEERE
Creative Teacher

More than anything else, passion for the Son of God has to be guarded and cultivated or we will lose it. I find that almost every good thing in my life is all too ready to compete for my time and intimacy with the Son of God.

Jack Deere

Jack describes his beginning this way: "When I was converted at seventeen years of age, I had no religious or church background of any kind. Immediately, I fell in love with the Lord Jesus. I began to devour His Word. I talked to Him constantly. I witnessed to every one of my non-Christian friends . . . I was so in love with Jesus that nothing else really mattered to me."

Jack's zeal led him to seminary, where he earned master's and doctorate degrees and eventually professorship at Dallas Theological Seminary. This was good, but not entirely good. He wrote about it this way: "In the process of getting theologically trained and becoming a seminary professor, I developed an intense passion for the precise study of the Word of God. Before I knew it, it happened again . . . I had put the Bible over the Lord Jesus, much like the Pharisees had put the law and their traditions above God."

More than any other thing, the turning point that laid bare this truth and rekindled his passion for God was a fresh discovery of God's Spirit and His power in Jack's life. Miracles, healings, the voice of God—these were all facets of the spiritual life that he had relegated to distant history. But history caught up with Jack and began to break into his comfortable little world in ways both exhilarating and intimidating.

"Somehow I knew I was at a crossroad in life, and that the way I responded to that voice [of the Spirit] would set a whole new direction for my life. I would either be moving closer to God or away from Him. I simply said, 'Yes, Lord.' That simple 'Yes' was the beginning of my learning again what it means to become like a child in the Kingdom of God."

𝕴 want passionate feelings to characterize my relationship with the Lord Jesus. Of course, I want to be perfectly obedient to the Lord, but I want the obedience to spring out of a passionate love for Him. I want to obey Jesus not simply out of discipline of duty, or because of some reward or fear of punishment. I want to serve Him simply for the joy of being able to please the One I love so much.

Jack Deere

wisdom from the now

Lord, make me a crisis man. Let me not be a mile-post on a single road, but make me a fork that men must turn one way or another in facing Christ in me.

Jim Elliot

Finding Your Way Home

Story is the most potent form of communication on the planet. Nothing connects with the human heart more, and nothing draws you closer to another person or raises your passion more powerfully than a story. That is largely why the movie and television industry wields such enormous influence upon society—they are in the storytelling business.

God is also in the storytelling business. The overwhelming bulk of the Bible is pure story—the accounts of people's successes and failures and their encounters with God. Jesus' ministry on the earth can be roughly divided into two activities: working miracles and telling stories.

In the New Rebellion, your greatest tool is your own story—the times and places where you have met God and God has met you, where heaven and earth have intersected within your life. The great opportunity of your lifetime is to invite others into God's story.

Your Story

127

1 the buzz

What's new in the realm of sharing your faith? Perhaps the best expression of it comes off the back cover of a recent book on evangelism by Brian McLaren.

"OUT: Evangelism as sales pitch, as conquest, as warfare, as ultimatum, as threat, as proof, as argument, as entertainment, as show, as monologue, as something you have to do.

"IN: Disciple-making as conversation, as friendship, as influence, as invitation, as companionship, as challenge, as opportunity, as dance, as something you get to do."

> **n†r**
>
> LORD, I will thank you with all my heart; I will sing to you before the gods. I will bow down facing your holy Temple, and I will thank you for your love and loyalty. You have made your name and your word greater than anything.
> Psalm 138:1–2 NCV

The *E*-word (*evangelism*) has struck fear in the hearts of earnest Christians for decades as many have grappled with a weighty guilt for not confronting more of their neighbors and coworkers in a good Christian mugging. The few that are brash enough to witness regularly take on a mystical aura of invincibility (whether their victims actually make it into the church community intact or not). The rest pray with furrowed brow for more commitment, diligently stalking their unbelieving friends for a chance to leap on them unawares with the *two-question test* or the *four spiritual laws*.

But that was then, and this is now. At least it is to be hoped that the church is moving beyond both the motivation and the methodology of the past. But both methods and motivations hinge upon mind-sets, and this is the crux: How do you understand the heart of God as expressed through the generations?

Every generation experiences a shift of values and expressions as compared to the previous generation; this is why the terms "builder," "boomer," and "buster" have been followed by "generation X," "generation Y," and "millennials," which have in turn been crowded by new terms like "twixters," "kidults," and "thresholders." Every micro-generation seems to have its own language, its own psychoses, its own clothing and music and legends. But if you pull off the macro lens and zoom out, you will find a seismic shift between the enlightenment mind-set and the new-generation mind-set.

> The new-generation mind conceives faith as more of a journey than a destination, more relational than cerebral, and ultimately as a story. Their story. God's story.

Without trying to dissect all the expressions of that shift, it's important to note its effect upon sharing faith. The new-generation mind conceives faith as more of a journey than a destination, more relational than cerebral, and ultimately as a story. Their story. God's story.

Sharing faith today is perhaps best understood as knowing where your story fits into God's redemptive story and then inviting others to find their place in God's story.

Your Story

the insight

Jesus was both a storyteller and a story-liver. As a storyteller, He constantly used word pictures to communicate eternal truths to His followers: The story of the prodigal son in Luke 15 speaks volumes on the nature of God and forgiveness; the story of the vine in John 15 highlights the mystical, intimate relationship you have with Jesus; the Kingdom parables of Matthew 13 penetrate some of the mysteries of heaven and its values.

> For Jesus, "sharing His faith" was not a canned, one-size-fits-all presentation.

As a story-liver, Jesus seemed to be always conscious of the Father's story of redemption and His own role in it. From village to village, He encountered hundreds and thousands of people. Implicit in His teaching and miracles was an invitation into a larger story. For Jesus, "sharing His faith" was not a canned, one-size-fits-all presentation. He read the minds and hearts of people and knew where their stories intersected God's story.

Let's look at a few examples. When a Pharisee named Nicodemus came secretly to Jesus at night, Jesus went right to the root issue for him—the need for personal humility in place of religious arrogance. He invited Nicodemus into God's story of spiritual rebirth, and the account leads one to believe that Nicodemus responded to it (see John 3).

When some men started tearing through the roof in order to lower a paralyzed man to where Jesus was teaching, Jesus responded to their initiative and invited the paralyzed man into restoration (see Mark 2). The story there is how the Kingdom of God restores someone from both the guilt of sin as well as physical brokenness. Jesus consistently read the situation and knew how to connect with a responsive heart.

In John 4, Jesus encountered a Samaritan woman at a well. The story was living water, and He used a "word of knowledge" to lay bare her heart. In a custom-crafted dialogue, Jesus got to the root issue in her heart—restoration from shame. And she responded exuberantly.

With the Gerasene demoniac of Mark 5, Jesus set the man free from the oppression of evil spirits, taking authority over the spiritual realm in order to restore the man's mind and ultimately redeem his life from the devastation of many years. The result was that the man wanted to follow Jesus as a disciple; instead, Jesus invited him to enlarge the story of redemption within in his own community.

Your Story

the point

Jesus appealed to men and women at the point of access: the mind of Nicodemus, the body of the paralytic, the heart of the Samaritan woman, and the spirit of the demoniac. He discerned the brokenness of their stories and breathed new hope for good endings. God is equipping you now to live fully in your own redemptive story, to discern the point of access in others, and to invite them into destiny in the story of God.

the talk

We must become aware of the difference between the most important need a person has and what that person feels is his most important need . . . When we pray for their felt needs and God answers, their eyes are opened to the reality and the power of God, and this in turn leads them to recognize their need for salvation.

ED SILVOSO

Out of a hundred men, one will read the Bible; the other ninety-nine will read the Christian.

D. L. MOODY

Preach the gospel every day; use words only when necessary.

SAINT FRANCIS OF ASSISI

> Knowing that we are fulfilling God's purpose is the only thing that really gives rest to the restless human heart.
>
> CHARLES COLSON

the word

Jesus said to his followers, "Go everywhere in the world, and tell the Good News to everyone."

Mark 16:15 NCV

When the Holy Spirit comes to you, you will receive power. You will be my witnesses—in Jerusalem, in all of Judea, in Samaria, and in every part of the world.

Acts 1:8 NCV

None of these things move me; nor do I count my life dear to myself, so that I may finish my race with joy, and the ministry which I received from the Lord Jesus, to testify to the gospel of the grace of God.

Acts 20:24 NKJV

We write you now about what has always existed, which we have heard, we have seen with our own eyes, we have looked at, and we have touched with our own hands. We write to you about the Word that gives life.

1 John 1:1 NCV

Peter and John answered and said to them, "Whether it is right in the sight of God to listen to you more than to God, you judge. For we cannot but speak the things which we have seen and heard."

Acts 4:19–20 NKJV

This is how much God loved the world: He gave his Son, his one and only Son. And this is why: so that no one need be destroyed; by believing in him, anyone can have a whole and lasting life. God didn't go to all the trouble of sending his Son merely to point an accusing finger, telling the world how bad it was. He came to help, to put the world right again. Anyone who trusts in him is acquitted.

John 3:16–18 MSG

Your Story

the your story tools

Read it . . .

Bruchko
Bruce Olson
God's impact upon the Motilone Indians of Columbia.

God's Beloved: A Spiritual Biography of Henri Nouwen
Michael O'Laughlin
A story of intimacy, brokenness, and friendship with Jesus.

Jack: The Life of C. S. Lewis
George Sayer
The definitive story of C. S. Lewis and how he changed contemporary Christianity.

Lifestyle Evangelism
Joe Aldrich
Developing a life that attracts seekers.

Mother Teresa
Kathryn Spink
From her childhood in the Balkans to her riveting service to the world's poor.

No Compromise
Melody Green
The gripping story of Keith Green and his impact on the world.

That None Should Perish
Ed Silvoso
A dramatic story of revival in Argentina through prayer.

Surf it . . .

www.goodseed.com
Resource to help you share God's story.

www.newchristendom.com
Reflections on current spiritual currents.

www.storytelling.com
Resources for improving storytelling skills.

Hear it . . .

Diverse City, Toby Mac

Every Move I Make, David Ruis

Everyone Is Beautiful, Waterdeep

The Father's Song, Matt Redman

Glo, Delirious

The Road to One Day, Passion

Spoken For, Mercy Me

Do it . . .

Leadership development for students, www.leadertreks.com.

Short-term mission opportunities to tell your story, www.owmjohn146.com.

Help translate "The Story," www.wycliffe.org.

TOP TEN

The Top Ten Ways to Tell Your Story

10 Keep a running journal of your journey with Jesus.

9 Share key turning points in your story with your close friends.

8 Look for the felt needs in people who live and work around you.

7 Look for people who are different from you—ethnically, socioeconomically, culturally—and listen to their stories and share yours.

6 In your relationships, don't just share truths; share your story of learning truth.

5 Consider how God interweaves your story with the stories of others.

4 Travel through third-world countries to enlarge your view of the human story.

3 Study the stories of biblical heroes to apply their lessons to your story.

2 Earn the right to speak by being a great listener.

1 As you share your story, always be respectful of other people's stories.

The Question

Does the love that God has for you compel you to tell others of His love for them?

Different reasons motivate people to tell God's story. Perhaps the most common, most internally destructive, and least effective is guilt. Others are motivated by spiritual ambition—a competitive desire to "win the lost," either for personal recognition within the church or by a sincere (but misguided) desire to win God's favor.

The biblical motivation for inviting others into God's story is love. The most well-known verse in the Bible opens with Jesus' words, "God so loved the world that He gave His only begotten Son" (John 3:16 NKJV). Paul stated in 2 Corinthians 5:14, "Christ's love has moved me to such extremes. His love has the first and last word in everything we do" (MSG). And 1 Corinthians 13 declares that the world's greatest eloquence, the most extensive wisdom and gifting, and the most supreme self-sacrifice are all *absolutely worthless without love* as the motivating force.

Most people you'll speak with are pretty tuned in to the motivations behind your sharing Christ. No one wants to be a project or a statistic. People want to be loved, and if they sense your love is genuine, most will be open to hearing and considering your story.

Interestingly enough, the opposite of love is not so often hate, but fear. This is why "perfect love casts out fear" (1 John 4:18 NKJV). Fear is the chief expression of an insecure love of self, and that misdirected love will absolutely stifle your ability to invite others into God's story.

> **I**nterestingly enough, the opposite of love is not so often hate, but fear. This is why "perfect love casts out fear."

If you never do share your love of Christ with others, then it's fair to ask yourself why. Afraid? Indifferent? Feel unable? The antidote is story: Your story has the ability to cut through intimidation in yourself and the defenses of others. You don't have to take any special evangelism course to tell your story. Your story is simply who you are.

What if there really are "angels" out there—not of the wings-and-halos type, but of the flesh-and-blood, laughter-and-tears type— people who are literally sent by God to intervene, to help those of us who have mucked up our lives, to give us a taste of grace?
Brian McLaren

Moved by God's Love

C. S. LEWIS
1898–1963

A young man who wishes to remain a sound Atheist cannot be too careful of his reading. There are traps everywhere—"Bibles laid open, millions of surprises," as Herbert says, "fine nets and stratagems." God is, if I may say it, very unscrupulous.

From C. S. Lewis's
Surprised by Joy

Clive Staples Lewis is perhaps the most beloved Christian figure of the twentieth century and the best-known advocate for orthodox Christianity. After Jesus and Paul, C. S. Lewis is the most-quoted author in Christian writings. And though his death is more than forty years past, his books continue to sell in ever-greater volume and his influence continues to soar.

Born in Belfast, Northern Ireland, into a very nominal Christian faith, his world was rocked by several pivotal events: the death of his mother when he was ten, an atheist tutor who grounded him in materialistic philosophy, and a World War I tour that killed his best friend. As Lewis (or "Jack" as he was known) left the military for Oxford University, he was decidedly agnostic toward God, yet a late-night conversation with two close friends—J. R. R.

Tolkien and Hugo Dyson—radically influenced his perspective. At a crucial point in the discussion, an unexpected wind surged through the trees and seemed to Jack to confirm a divine presence.

As the "Hound of Heaven" crept up on Jack, the struggle intensified. Personal disappointment with God was reluctant to give way to the intellectual integrity that pushed Jack toward belief. The story goes that Jack went for a drive one day, leaving as an agnostic and returning as a deist. The question of God was strangely and surprisingly settled for him.

With joy and zeal, Jack began to write and write and write, delighting the evangelicals of his day but earning the animosity of the fashionable liberals. Not characterized only by an extraordinary thinking, he wrote for the common people rather than the academic elite, shunning religious jargon and utilizing the bold everyday language of a post-Christian world.

He was a master storyteller who wrote children's books, science fiction, and intellectual and popular works. He told his story in two autobiographies. But more than that, he helped people understand God's story—and their own story—with unparalleled clarity. Almost forty books bore his name before he died of heart and kidney failure November 22, 1963. His legacy endures.

wisdom from the past

The word of God is like a mirror in that it shows us who we really are. It is like a map because it shows us where we need to go. It is like a portrait for it paints for us a picture of who God is.

David Wallace

The God Who Speaks

It must not be taken for granted that, in His essence, God is a God who speaks. Who communicates. Isn't that extraordinary? He's not silent or removed, but engages us and invites us into true relationship through His words. He created—not just static trophies of His power—but creatures in His own image, capable of great passion and communication.

Someone has said, "Words have the power to take precious objects out of the closet of the soul and share them with another soul." This isn't just true with people; it's true with God. He opened His heart to Adam and Eve, to Abel, to Abraham, and to thousands after them. What we call "the Word" is simply a record of His interactions with His men and women. And nothing delights His heart more than when His people open up their hearts to Him in intimate interaction.

God's Word

the buzz

So what's new to say about something that's been going on for thousands of years? God has been speaking—some listen and others don't. But that's not the whole story.

There is in the New Rebellion generation a growing awareness of when, where, and how God speaks. Some people in previous generations understood the precious value of the Bible. But in elevating the Bible, they wound up reducing the God of the Bible to modern muteness. In other words, they thought this: He spoke in biblical times, but He doesn't anymore. And this: He used to interact personally and intimately with His people, but now all we have is the manual. This way of thinking was a serious mistake.

The Bible is the clearest, most trustworthy revelation and measure of God's character. It is the authoritative representation of His heart for you. But it is not all of God's heart for you—He continues to pour forth constant streams of wisdom and guidance for your life. In absolute consistency with the Scriptures (and frequently *through* the Scriptures), your heavenly Father intends to walk through your days in intimate fellowship with you.

In the past God spoke to our ancestors through the prophets many times and in many different ways. But now in these last days God has spoken to us through his Son.
Hebrews 1:1–2 NCV

If God's overarching concern is for His people to agree with a statement of belief, then you don't need *Him;* all you need is a creed. But that would never content His heart or yours! Right belief does not change the world. Correct doctrine does not usher in the Kingdom of heaven. Your destiny hinges upon a passionate and personal relationship—which is the whole purpose of God's Word.

The New Rebellion—that collection of passionate believers who confront the world's misguided agenda with God's redemptive agenda—is powered by this caliber of relationship. These believers are initiated by relationship and known by relationship. When they read the Scriptures, they hear God's voice echoing personally to them. They depend upon God's Spirit to illuminate and activate those words within them. They listen intently to His voice and then walk it out in trusting obedience.

> The Bible is the clearest, most trustworthy revelation and measure of God's character. It is the authoritative representation of His heart for you.

God's Word flows through everything He has made—His world, His people, even your own spirit. He speaks through art, through music, through movies, through life experiences. He speaks through the wise and the foolish, through the devout and the unbelieving. He even spoke through a donkey once (see Numbers 22).

The charge to people today is the same as it was in Jesus' time: "He who has ears to hear, let him hear!" (Mark 4:9 NKJV). But here's the point: It will be only those who know His *heart* who will rightly discern His *words*.

God's Word

the insight

There are two very compelling passages from God's Word that illumine the connection between the Word of God and the God of the Word. One comes from an apostle, one who had unique intimacy with and insight into Jesus. The second comes from an ancient king in Israel a thousand years earlier.

> Jesus came to speak, with His words and with His life, about the Kingdom—about the King, about the culture of heaven, and about your place in that Kingdom. **ntr**

The disciple John wrote these mysteriously penetrating words: "In the beginning there was the Word. The Word was with God, and the Word was God. He was with God in the beginning. All things were made by him, and nothing was made without him. In him there was life, and that life was the light of all people" (John 1:1–4 NCV).

John, the disciple who knew Jesus best, saw that Christ was the ultimate Word that God had ever spoken, the ultimate communication from heaven to planet Earth. God is not content to speak from afar but determined to get close and personal in your life. This was—and is—Jesus' job. Jesus came to speak, with His words and with His life, about the Kingdom—about the King, about the culture of heaven, and about your place in that Kingdom.

And Jesus' job continues through the operation of God's Spirit. Jesus continues to be the Word of God, spoken and amplified and clarified and delivered straight into your heart so you will know Him. And partner with Him in changing this earth for Him.

A second penetrating insight comes from King Solomon. Long before Christ would incarnate Himself in human flesh, Christ incarnated Himself as Wisdom. The role was the same: to communicate the heart of the Father.

Read Solomon's description:

"The LORD brought me forth as the first of his works, before his deeds of old; I was appointed from eternity, from the beginning, before the world began . . . Then I was the craftsman at his side. I was filled with delight day after day . . . rejoicing in his whole world and delighting in mankind. Now then, my sons, listen to me; blessed are those who keep my ways" (selections from Proverbs 8 NIV).

Notice the striking similarity between John 1 and Proverbs 8. They are both descriptions of the way Jesus participated in the Creation and continues to communicate the wisdom of God. Creation was the expression of God's spoken word, and that creative word continues to bring light and life into your relationship with God today.

God's Word

the point

In Proverbs, Wisdom is not just a body of knowledge. Wisdom is an expression of Christ; she is personified as a woman worthy of your pursuit. Wisdom pours out her Spirit on you, divulging all that she knows (see 1:23). She keeps you from wrong choices and painful lessons (see 9:4–6). She calls you away from failure and destruction and toward integrity and purity (see 9:10–18). She helps you safely fulfill your God-given destiny (see 8:34–36). Wisdom embraces those who embrace the words of God.

the talk

Who can endure a doctrine which would allow only dentists to say whether our teeth were aching, only cobblers to say whether our shoes hurt us, and only governments to tell us whether we were being well governed?

C. S. LEWIS

Never let good books take the place of the Bible. Drink from the Well, not from the streams that flow from the Well.

AMY CARMICHAEL

I have known ninety-five of the world's great men in my time, and of these, eighty-seven were followers of the Bible. The Bible is stamped with a Specialty of Origin, and an immeasurable distance separates it from all competitors.

W. E. GLADSTONE

Whatever merit there is in anything that I have written is simply due to the fact that when I was a child my mother daily read me a part of the Bible and daily made me learn a part of it by heart.

JOHN RUSKIN

the word

Every word of God is pure; He is a shield to those who put their trust in Him. Do not add to His words, lest He rebuke you, and you be found a liar.

Proverbs 30:5–6 NKJV

The same thing is true of the words I speak. They will not return to me empty. They make the things happen that I want to happen, and they succeed in doing what I send them to do.

Isaiah 55:11 NCV

I have restrained my feet from every evil way, that I may keep Your word. I have not departed from Your judgments, for You Yourself have taught me. How sweet are Your words to my taste, sweeter than honey to my mouth! Through Your precepts I get understanding: therefore I hate every false way. Your word is a lamp to my feet and a light to my path.

Psalm 119:101–105 NKJV

Let the teaching of Christ live in you richly. Use all wisdom to teach and instruct each other by singing psalms, hymns, and spiritual songs with thankfulness in your hearts to God. Everything you do or say should be done to obey Jesus your Lord. And in all you do, give thanks to God the Father through Jesus.

Colossians 3:16–17 NCV

All Scripture is given by God and is useful for teaching, for showing people what is wrong in their lives, for correcting faults, and for teaching how to live right. Using the Scriptures, the person who serves God will be capable, having all that is needed to do every good work.

2 Timothy 3:16–17 NCV

God's Word

the God's Word tools

Read it . . .

The Bible Jesus Read
Philip Yancey
Discovering the Old Testament in light
of the New.

The Bible Made Easy
Mark Waters
Simple pocket guide to Bible facts and
stories.

The Evidence Bible
Ray Comfort
Collection of tools to defend the
authenticity of God's Word.

Grasping God's Word
Duvall, Hays, and Vanhoozer
A hands-on approach to reading, inter-
preting, and applying the Bible.

**How to Read the Bible for All It's
Worth**
Gordon D. Fee and Douglas Stuart
Illumination of the various kinds of
literature in God's Word.

The Incomparable Christ
John Stott
A portrait of Jesus from both Scripture
and history.

**Reflections on the Bible: Human
Word and Word of God**
Dietrich Bonhoeffer
Essays from one of the twentieth
century's great thinkers.

Surf it . . .

www.bibles-for-the-world.com
Bible translations in over thirty
languages.

www.bibleworld.info
Tools and links for God's Word.

www.jesusfolk.com
Weaving the Word with the Web.

www.praize.com
An all-in-one Christian online community.

Hear it . . .

Advent of a Miracle, Strongarm

Be the Word, Clay Crosse

Fault Is History, Souljahz

Loud and Clear, O C Supertones

The Night We Called It a Day,
Deepspace 5

Philmore, Philmore

Red Letter Day, Newsong

Do it . . .

**An online concordance to search for
Bible verses**, www.biblegateway.com.

**Bible retreats and conferences in
northeastern Pennsylvania**,
www.montrosebible.org.

**Daily readings to cover God's Word
in a year**, www.oneyearbibleonline.com.

The Top Ten
Scriptures to Memorize

10 "God can do much, much more than anything we can ask" (Ephesians 3:20 NCV).

9 "The Spirit produces the fruit of love, joy, peace, patience, kindness, goodness, faithfulness, gentleness, self-control" (Galatians 5:22–23 NCV).

8 "Think about the things that are true and honorable and right" (Philippians 4:8 NCV).

7 "I have taken your words to heart so I would not sin against you" (Psalm 119:11 NCV).

6 "Troubles test your faith, and this will give you patience" (James 1:3 NCV).

5 "Do not worry about anything, but pray and ask God for everything" (Philippians 4:6 NCV).

4 "If we live in the light, as God is in the light, we can share fellowship with each other" (1 John 1:7 NCV).

3 "The people who trust the LORD will become strong again" (Isaiah 40:31 NCV).

2 "He makes sure that justice is done, and he protects those who are loyal to him" (Proverbs 2:8 NCV).

1 "I am the vine, and you are the branches" (John 15:5 NCV).

The Question

- ->

When you're read-

ing the Bible, can

you tell when God

is actually speak-

ing to you?

He wrote it all, right? And He wrote it all for your benefit. But there are times when the words just seem to leap off the page, when you know that God put you in just the right passage on just the right day to say something important to you! The Bible is always good, but sometimes it's GOOD!

But other times, you're not so sure. Sometimes the words feel dry and irrelevant to your life that day. Is God speaking then?

One thing is for sure: God is always talking. He doesn't always answer the questions you're asking, at least not when you're asking them. Sometimes He knows you need some time and space before you're ready to hear a particular answer. But He's always talking, and He's always inviting you into His confidence and into His heart. That's just the God He is.

Consider these skills for listening to God in the Scriptures. *Place yourself in the passage.* Whether it's Old Testament or New, history or poetry, take the situation or topic and superimpose it over your life. Are there any correlations? Any implicit challenges or affirmations?

Pray the Scriptures. Grab the heart of God as it's revealed in that passage and pray it into your life. If it's an encouraging passage from the life of a great biblical hero, consider how God may be teaching you similar things. If it's a story of great failure, ask God to highlight any traces of that deficiency within your own soul. If it's a song of praise, make it your song. If it's insight, make it your truth.

One thing is for sure: God is always talking.

Learn to listen, take time to wait and ponder, pray God's heart, and hear His voice that comes to you today.

If the reader understands very little of the
word of God, he ought to read it very much;
for the Spirit explains the word by the word . . .
The frequent reading of the Scriptures creates a
delight in them, so that the more we read them,
the more we desire to do so.
George Müller

The Ancient Word for Today's Generation →

JOHN FISCHER
Artist with a Message

We [are] somehow expecting the text itself to balance out the worldliness of the day and make us into a "good Christian family." But if we don't give thought to what we hear, what good is the hearing?

John Fischer

"An artist, thinker, communicator driven to create and personally deliver a message of deeper understanding of God, confirming those seeking a faith that intersects the real world." That is the way Fischer describes himself. And he's been at it for almost three decades—grappling with the unchanging realities of God and their application in a constantly changing world.

Fischer recorded his first album in the late sixties—*The Cold Cathedral*—as an overflow of the spiritual renewal taking place then. After college, he began a ministry mentorship where he began to develop his own blend of humor, writing, speaking, and music that has produced twelve albums and eleven books. In short, Fischer is driven to communicate the Word of God. But he also understands the pitfalls.

"The Pharisees made it their job,"

Fischer wrote, "to study and know the Scriptures in order to gain the upper hand on the things of God and keep the rest of the people in the dark. For the Pharisees, the Scriptures had ceased to be a form of revelation. 'Manipulation' better describes their use of the sacred texts. By them they engineered and justified their own righteousness, and by them they controlled others . . .

"Because we are all prone to pharisaical attitudes, we'd be wise to check for any of these tendencies in our own lives and ministries. By determining where the Pharisees went wrong in their handling of Scripture, we can make sure we are not inadvertently traveling a similar path."

> John Fischer pushes and pulls. He pushes us out to new borders of faith while always pulling us back to the centrality of Christ.
>
> Jay Kesler, president of Taylor University

This is the kind of gentle provocation that characterizes Fischer's dialogue. He challenges people's religious attitudes and behaviors but without iconoclastic harshness. Instead, he draws you winsomely into the meaning of the gospel.

Fischer and his wife, Marti, now make their home in Laguna Beach, California, where they continue to grapple with and communicate the heart of the Scriptures.

wisdom from the now

Jesus says that the root of anxiety is inadequate faith in our Father's future grace. As unbelief gets the upper hand in our hearts, one of the effects is anxiety. The root cause of anxiety is a failure to trust all that God has promised to be for us in Jesus.

John Piper

A Life of Trusting Obedience

The concept of faith is a mysterious one. You hear people use the term in different ways: "She's a person of faith." "After his wife died, he lost his faith." "If you're going to pray for healing, you've got to have faith." So what exactly is this thing called faith?

At its core, faith is just a *trusting obedience*. Its power comes from the object of your faith: God. The reason faith is such a key issue in God's purposes is that it describes the dynamic of bringing your will into alignment with the will of heaven, and this is powerful indeed.

Your own will has the power to affect a small sphere: yourself and the people in close proximity to you. But that won't change the planet. God's will, on the other hand, can. And it will when your life becomes a channel of it.

Faith

1 the buzz

The first thing to understand about faith is that it's an essential quality in the Christian journey. Faith is not just for the spiritually elite. God expects every son and daughter to experience faith and live in its reality. Paul revealed in Romans 14:23 NIV that "everything that does not come from faith is sin," and Hebrews 11:6 NIV states that "without faith it is impossible to please God." So, whatever else you may learn here, the New Rebellion is anchored within this conviction: Faith is available to all, and faith is required to walk in relationship with God. But let's get practical. How does faith really work? Here are three important ways.

I am not ashamed, for I know whom I have believed and am persuaded that He is able to keep what I have committed to Him until that Day.
2 Timothy 1:12 NKJV

Faith responds to the person of Jesus and His revealed will. A familiar verse says, "So faith comes from hearing the Good News, and people hear the Good News when someone tells them about Christ" (Romans 10:17 NCV). This means that your faith is initiated through a personal encounter with Jesus; in His presence, you become aware of His will ("the Good News"), and faith springs up inside you with the desire and ability to trust that message and obey Him.

Faith acts largely through your spiritual gifts. Romans 12 makes an intriguing connection between your faith and your gifting. In the first two verses, Paul set the stage, urging you to become a "living sacrifice"—completely aligned with the will of God. Then verse 3 says, "Think of yourself with sober judgment, in accordance with the measure of faith God has given you" (NIV).

How do you put that faith into motion? Through your spiritual gifts! In verses 4–8, God describes many of the gifts He plants within people, and He encourages you to come into partnership with Him. God prophesies; you prophesy. God serves; you serve. God teaches; you teach. Can you see it?

Faith activates the promises of God. Faith is your catalyst to unlock and release God's intentions in the earth. When Jesus was here physically, He described how people's faith released healing into people's bodies (Mark 5:34; 10:52). He described how faith released salvation (Luke 7:50). Romans 4 contains a lengthy discussion about Abraham and how his faith unlocked the grace of salvation for him and all who would follow him.

> The New Rebellion is anchored within this conviction: Faith is available to all, and faith is required to walk in relationship with God.

The writer of Hebrews challenged every generation to "imitate those who through faith and patience inherit what has been promised" (6:12 NIV). This is an unstoppable combination in your life: Trusting obedience combined with a persevering patience will inevitably birth God's promised intentions in and through you. Believe it!

Faith

the insight

In the "faith chapter" of Hebrews 11, the honor roll of heroes ends with this statement: "I do not have time to tell about Gideon, Barak, Samson, Jephthah, David, Samuel and the prophets, who through faith conquered kingdoms . . . whose weakness was turned to strength; and who became powerful in battle" (verses 32–34 NIV). One of the stories that was left out—the story of Gideon—will now be told.

> Faith responded to the person and message of God. Faith acted through the spiritual gifts. And then faith activated God's promise.

The nation of Israel had been under the oppressive thumb of Midian for seven long years. Both the land and the souls of the people lay in shambles when the angel of God showed up at Gideon's place with an absurd promise: "The LORD is with you, mighty warrior . . . It will seem as if the Midianites you are fighting are only one man" (Judges 6:12, 16 NCV).

Gideon's first response was far short of faith. First, disappointment and bitterness, followed by the request for proof of identity—a miraculous sign. But this encounter with God awakened faith in Gideon's heart, and in worship he aligned himself with the will of God.

The trusting obedience of faith? He took ten men and tore down the altar of Baal and the Asherah pole—the local idols that precipitated God's judgment. The risk of this obedience was very real as he narrowly escaped being lynched by the raging townspeople. But Gideon's faith was only just beginning to flow.

Faith flowed next through Gideon's spiritual gift of leadership as he summoned an army of 32,000 Israelites to face the Midianites. An impressive number, but only a fraction of the enemy's army! Again, faith requires trust and obedience, and Gideon moved in unprecedented courage to trim his army down by 22,000 and then by another 9,700. Can you even call 300 men an army?

Can you see the pattern? *Faith responded* to the person and message of God. *Faith acted* through the spiritual gifts. And then *faith activated* God's promise—the promise that He would deliver Israel by a "mighty warrior" from its oppression. After an unimpressive start, Gideon showed himself willing to trust and obey the commands of God, no matter how preposterous.

Gideon's final plan was the most preposterous of all. Surrounding the enemy's camp at night, his 300 men broke pitchers, lit their torches, and yelled. That's it! As a result, the enemy killed themselves in mass confusion, and God's bold promise was delivered.

Faith

the point

The mysterious wisdom of God shows itself in some unlikely ways—in partnership, in weakness, in trust, and in obedience. These qualities add up to a life of faith, and nothing moves the heart and Kingdom of God like it. God intends to marry His strength and your weakness, and faith is what activates the divine connection. This is your invitation. This is the call of greatness upon your life.

the talk

To one who has faith, no explanation is necessary. To one without faith, no explanation is possible.

SAINT THOMAS AQUINAS

The essence of faith is being satisfied with all that God is for us in Jesus.

JOHN PIPER

Faith is the art of holding on to things your reason has once accepted in spite of your changing moods.

C. S. LEWIS

Fear can keep us up all night long, but faith makes one fine pillow.

ANONYMOUS

the word

When Jesus heard this, he was amazed. He said to those who were following him, "I tell you the truth, this is the greatest faith I have found, even in Israel."

Matthew 8:10 NCV

People receive God's promise by having faith. This happens so the promise can be a free gift. Then all of Abraham's children can have that promise. It is not only for those who live under the law of Moses but for anyone who lives with faith like that of Abraham, who is the father of us all.

Romans 4:16 NCV

We are always confident, knowing that while we are at home in the body we are absent from the Lord. For we walk by faith, not by sight.

2 Corinthians 5:6 NKJV

When we are in Christ Jesus, it is not important if we are circumcised or not. The important thing is faith—the kind of faith that works through love.

Galatians 5:6–7 NCV

Whatever is not from faith is sin.

Romans 14:23 NKJV

Faith

the faith tools

Read it . . .

After the Locusts
Jan Coleman
Encouragement for women who have suffered loss.

The Case for Faith
Lee Strobel
Convincing answers to the tough questions of faith.

Disappointment with God
Philip Yancey
Probing the hidden nature of God.

Future Grace
John Piper
A trusting anticipation of encountering God's grace on the journey.

Mere Christianity
C. S. Lewis
Modern classic on core Christian thought.

Ruthless Trust
Brennan Manning
Exploring the secret to living fully in the love of God.

Simple Faith
Charles Swindoll
Freedom from performance-driven Christianity.

Surf it . . .

www.answersingenesis.org
Reasons for faith in the Creation story.

www.christian-faith.com
Some perspectives on following Jesus.

www.wagnerleadership.org
Courses and resources to build your faith.

Hear it . . .

Faith, Jason Upton

Fashion Expo Round One, Fashion Expo

Much Afraid, Jars of Clay

Nothing Is Sound, Switchfoot

Our Love Is Loud, Passion

Rock of Ages . . . Hymns & Faith, Amy Grant

Underground Rise: Sunrise/Sunset, Various

Do it . . .

Hone your skills to communicate your faith in writing,
www.faithmania.com.

Video series on aspects of faith,
www.nooma.com.

The Top Ten Places in Life That Require Trust

10 Prayer—knowing that He's there and hears every word. Even the ones you haven't said.

9 Friendships—knowing that He can sustain the ones that matter.

8 Parents—knowing that He can bring understanding and respect.

7 Children—knowing that they are held by stronger arms than yours.

6 Church—knowing that God is bigger than problems and messes.

5 Personality—knowing that He is changing you and unlocking your true self.

4 Career—knowing that God is preparing you for important things.

3 Finances—knowing that God is absolutely committed to your supply.

2 Destiny—knowing that your journey has a good destination.

1 Your life—knowing that God will finish what He started!

The Question

Do you believe that God can take away the thing you most despise in yourself?

Have you gotten honest enough with yourself to know that part of yourself you most wish you could change? The one thing that you desperately desire God to take away? To replace? To transform? Can you name it?

Now, does that thing feel completely removed from the realm of faith? It isn't, you know. Faith encompasses all your life—from loneliness to an embarrassing stutter to extreme shyness and insecurity. A bad temper, you say? Faith's got you covered. A dead-end career? Faith is the key to unlock the purposes of God in your life.

First, ask God to reveal His purposes. Every obstacle and every place of shame or frustration is an invitation into the heart of God—to know His passion for you, to become the man or woman you're meant to be, to break through hindrances and live a purposeful life.

Second, you must trust. To accept His unconditional love and commitment to you. To know that He will never let you go and never turn loose of your future. Trust is a confidence in God's affection for you that cannot be beaten out of you by time and difficulty. Trust outlasts the tests in your life. Trust overcomes confusion and disappointment.

Third, embrace the goodwill of God in your life and obey the things He's telling you to do. Search for Him in the Scriptures. Find and apply everything He has to say about your area of struggle. Pray through the issues, and don't give up. Often, your freedom comes in layers like an onion. One layer of freedom at a time. But it comes only to the person who knows God and lives out his or her trusting obedience. The life of faith.

> **F**aith is the key to unlock the purposes of God in your life.

I would mention that the Lord very graciously gave me, from the very commencement of my [salvation], a measure of simplicity and childlike disposition in spiritual things, so that while I was exceedingly ignorant of the Scriptures, and was still from time to time overcome even by outward sins, yet I was enabled to carry most minute matters to the Lord in prayer.
George Müeller

Extreme Faith

GEORGE MÜELLER

1805–1898

I desire to expound the Holy Scriptures regularly to a thousand orphans, instead of doing so to 300. I desire that it may be yet more abundantly manifest that God is still the Hearer and Answerer of prayer, and that He is the living God now as He ever was and ever will be.

Journal entry
December 26, 1850

Among the greatest monuments of what can be accomplished through simple faith in God are the great orphanages covering thirteen acres of ground on Ashley Downs, Bristol, England," wrote J. Gilchrist Lawson. Born in the kingdom of Prussia at the rise of the nineteenth century, George Müeller's early life was characterized by compulsive lying and stealing, even while attending seminary. But God had other plans.

In Müeller's own words: "My friend Beta . . . was in the habit of going on Saturday evenings to the house of a Christian, where there was a meeting . . . They read the Bible, sang, prayed, and read a printed sermon. No sooner had I heard this, but it was to me as if I had found something after which I had been seeking all my life long." That evening was a turning point—an encounter with the love and grace of God that marked him forever after.

After several bouts of severe illness, Müeller began evangelistic church-planting in 1832. A couple of years later he started a charity called Scripture Knowledge Institution for Home and Abroad, out of which flowed his most famous ministry—to orphans. This charity became the vehicle for channeling more than seven million dollars into aid to the poor, to schools, to missionaries, and to evangelism, all without ever asking a soul for a dime. Müeller came to the conviction that God alone was his source, and his prayer life became the anchor for all personal and ministry provision.

"At the time of Mr. Müeller's death 122,000 persons had been taught in the schools supported by these funds; and about 282,000 Bibles and 1,500,000 Testaments had been distributed by means of the same fund. Also 112,000,000 religious books, pamphlets and tracts had been circulated; missionaries had been aided in all parts of the world; and no less than ten thousand orphans had been cared for by means of this same fund," Lawson wrote.

wisdom from the past

Our authority comes out of who
we are in Christ, and our capacity to
intimidate the enemy comes out of
our intimacy with God.

Graham Cooke

A Powerful Partnership

The danger of becoming too focused upon your spiritual enemy is exceeded only by the danger of ignoring him. Jesus did neither. Instead, He went about His Father's business of bringing a radical redemption to an oppressed world while maintaining a vivid clarity of the spiritual warfare operating around Him.

His redemptive work of loving, healing, and teaching was set within a larger framework—forcefully advancing His Kingdom. His message was consistent: The Kingdom of heaven is near you. And the very message that brought hope to His generation brought horror to His enemy, because the enemy knew that the enlargement of God's Kingdom automatically meant the destruction of his.

Your mission is to continue and to enlarge the work of Christ. You "do the same things that I do," Jesus says. "[You] will do even greater things than these, because I am going to the Father" (John 14:12 NCV).

Warfare

1 the buzz

How, exactly, do you extend the work of Christ to advance His Kingdom and put the enemy to flight? By understanding and correctly handling three key principles: jurisdiction, authority, and power.

Let's begin with some definitions. *Jurisdiction* is your invitation to rule a particular domain. *Authority* is your right to rule, which is released through intimate partnership. *Power* is your ability to rule and enforce your authority.

God invites you—indeed, requires you—to rule certain areas of your life and to rule them well. The first jurisdiction was entrusted to Adam and Eve with the charge to "be fruitful and increase in number; fill the earth and subdue it. Rule over the fish of the sea and the birds of the air and over every living creature that moves on the ground" (Genesis 1:28 NIV). That mandate is now yours.

We fight with weapons that are different from those the world uses. Our weapons have power from God that can destroy the enemy's strong places.
2 Corinthians 10:4 NCV

Practically speaking, your mandate probably includes at least three important spheres—your *home*, your *work*, and your *church*. It's vital that you understand your God-given jurisdiction in each sphere and recognize that jurisdiction is always entrusted to a community, never to solitary individuals. Which paves the way for authority.

God sets you into relationships that are essential for ruling well within your home, your work, and your church, but it's up to you to build a unified purpose in each arena. If you are single, your partnership begins with God and extends to the people He brings into your spheres of jurisdiction. If you are married, that intimate partnership then becomes the basis of your authority in every arena—both inside the home and out.

When the invitation to rule (jurisdiction) finds an able partnership to rule (authority), the result is power—the ability to rule and enforce your authority. This is true in the natural realm as well as the spiritual. This is where God backs you up and brings the power necessary to rule well. When power is understood to be the domain of God, then wise men and women cease to grasp for it and instead embrace a life of trusting obedience, just as Jesus taught and practiced.

> God sets you into relationships that are essential for ruling well within your home, your work, and your church, but it's up to you to build a unified purpose in each arena.

God has called you to live in His power in every area. As you come into unity with your spouse in the home, God will release His power to love and lead your family. As you build unity with coworkers, God will empower your projects with heavenly wisdom and effectiveness. Together with your church leadership, God will anoint your spiritual gifts to inspire others in their pursuit of Him. This is how you win spiritual battles.

Warfare

the insight

A passage in Luke 10 opens an amazing window into Jesus' engagement in spiritual warfare and highlights how He will equip you to carry on that important task. It's a crucial crossroads in Jesus' ministry. He personally proclaimed and demonstrated His emerging Kingdom. He equipped His twelve disciples to do the same. Then He knew He had to enlarge the circle and empower another dimension of ministry, and so He commissioned seventy-two more.

> Stay focused on the main thing—not your spiritual power, not your enemy, but upon your intimate relationship with Jesus.

Here is how it unfolded.

The Strategy. Verse 1 says that He sent them out in teams of two. Don't overlook the essential value of partnership that was established for effective warfare.

The Jurisdiction. "Go! I am sending you out like lambs among wolves" (verse 3 NIV). That was the invitation. That was the call to engage the adversary, to displace him and establish God's rule instead.

The Mission. "Heal the sick who are there and tell them, 'The kingdom of God is near you'" (verse 9 NIV). Your mission will always include a combination of declaring and demonstrating the Kingdom purposes of God, just as the seventy-two did.

The Results. Joy and power. Verse 17 says that Jesus' disciples returned with joy, and verse 21 highlights Jesus' great joy in response. But the real result was the release of spiritual authority and power that caused the mission itself to succeed. Jesus said, "I saw Satan fall like lightning from heaven. I have given you authority to . . . overcome all the power of the enemy" (verses 18–19 NIV).

Partnership began with each disciple's personal attachment to Jesus and His mission. It was then compounded by the teams-of-two strategy that brought them into an extremely focused unity. That unity released the authority that in turn released the power of God to dethrone Satan in their region and establish a Kingdom presence there.

The Focal Point. Jesus offered another important lesson in relation to spiritual warfare: "Do not rejoice that the spirits submit to you, but rejoice that your names are written in heaven" (verse 20 NIV). In other words, stay focused on the main thing—not your spiritual power, not your enemy, but upon your intimate relationship with Jesus. That is the source of your life and power. Jesus continued (verse 22) to revel in the intimate partnership He experienced with the Father . . . and in which He included you.

Warfare

the point

Paul reminded the Ephesians that "our fight is not against people on earth but against . . . the spiritual powers of evil in the heavenly world" (Ephesians 6:12 NCV). The New Rebellion includes warring against a spiritual enemy. The good news is that "all authority has been given to Me in heaven and on earth. Go therefore and make disciples of all" (Matthew 28:18–19 NKJV). Knowing that you have been well equipped with the jurisdiction, authority, and power to be a world-changer, you can engage the mission of making disciples.

the talk

Jesus was manifested to destroy the works of the devil. How do we destroy the works of the devil? We must manifest Jesus! The basis of our credibility is Christ revealed in and through us!

REUVEN DORON

God judged it better to bring good out of evil than to suffer no evil to exist.

SAINT AUGUSTINE OF HIPPO

Victory is the normal experience of a Christian; defeat should be the abnormal experience.

WATCHMAN NEE

The devil is not terribly frightened of our human efforts and credentials. But he knows his kingdom will be damaged when we begin to lift up our hearts to God.

JIM CYMBALA

the word

Be sober, be vigilant; because your adversary the devil walks about like a roaring lion, seeking whom he may devour. Resist him.

1 Peter 5:8–9 NKJV

"Be angry, and do not sin": do not let the sun go down on your wrath, nor give place to the devil.

Ephesians 4:26–27 NKJV

The thief does not come except to steal, and to kill, and to destroy. I have come that they may have life, and that they may have it more abundantly.

John 10:10 NKJV

Behold, I give you the authority to trample on serpents and scorpions, and over all the power of the enemy, and nothing shall by any means hurt you.

Luke 10:19 NKJV

Be strong in the Lord and in his great power. Put on the full armor of God so that you can fight against the devil's evil tricks. Our fight is not against people on earth but against the rulers and authorities and the powers of this world's darkness, against the spiritual powers of evil in the heavenly world. That is why you need to put on God's full armor.

Ephesians 6:10–13 NCV

Then he showed me Joshua, the high priest, standing in front of the LORD's angel. And Satan was standing by Joshua's right side to accuse him.

Zechariah 3:1 NCV

Warfare

the warfare tools

Read it . . .

Bondage Breaker
Neil Anderson
Throwing off sin and strongholds.

Clean House, Strong House
Kimberly Daniels
Understanding spiritual warfare, demonic strongholds, and deliverance.

Free in Christ
Pablo Bottari
Principles for spiritual deliverance.

Lord, Is It Warfare?
Teach Me to Stand
Kay Arthur
Practical battle tactics for daily living.

Servant Warfare
Steve Sjogren
The spiritual power of kindness.

Taking Our Cities for God
John Dawson
Strategies for breaking community strongholds.

That None Should Perish
Ed Silvoso
The power and results of prayer evangelism.

The Warfare of the Spirit
A. W. Tozer
Classic devotional on God's authority.

Surf it . . .

www.spirithome.com/spirwarf.html
Practical answers to questions on spiritual warfare.

www.spiritual-warfare.net
Teaching, testimonies, and resources on warfare.

www.thearmorofgod.com
Bracelets with Ephesians 6 charms.

Hear it . . .

Awaken, Natalie Grant

Can You Hear Us?, David Crowder

Instruments of Faith and Victory, Various

The Other Side, Billy Ray Cyrus

Songs of Warfare and Battle, Various

Storm, Fernando Ortega

Summer of Darkness, Demon Hunter

Do it . . .

Conferences on spiritual warfare, www.globalharvestministries.org.

Warfare through world missions, www.namb.net.

Join focused prayer initiatives, www.watchmannetwork.org.

Blog on spiritual warfare www.battleinchrist.blogsport.com.

TOP TEN

The Top Ten Weapons of War

10 Self-control and vigilance: "Control yourselves and be careful!" (1 Peter 5:8 NCV).

9 Obedience: "Our weapons have power from God" (2 Corinthians 10:4 NCV).

8 Confidence and perseverance: "You must hold on, so you can do what God wants" (Hebrews 10:36 NCV).

7 The Word of God: "God's word is alive and working and is sharper than a double-edged sword" (Hebrews 4:12 NCV).

6 Justice: "The rider on the horse is called Faithful and True, and he is right when he judges" (Revelation 19:11 NCV).

5 Worship: "Your offering must be only for God and pleasing to him" (Romans 12:1 NCV).

4 Truth: "Stand strong, with the belt of truth tied around your waist" (Ephesians 6:14 NCV).

3 Prayer: "Pray in the Spirit at all times" (Ephesians 6:18 NCV).

2 Faith: "Be alert. Continue strong in the faith" (1 Corinthians 16:13 NCV).

1 Love: "I say to you, love your enemies" (Matthew 5:44 NCV).

The Question

In the warfare over planet Earth, the enemy's chief weapons are lies. When his lies are believed, it leads to sin. This war has many casualties—sometimes you may be one of them; sometimes it may be someone you love. Sometimes pain is deserved, and sometimes it isn't. Sin has brought suffering into the world, and that suffering affects everyone.

The real damage of sin is that the consequences don't just affect the person who sinned—all those within that person's jurisdiction are affected. Your sin affects your spouse or your parents or your children or all of them. Your sin affects your extended family and even your church family. At one level it affects the entire human family. What remains are intersecting circles of suffering in the world. Sometimes you're the victim, and sometimes you're the perpetrator.

What do you think about God when bad things happen to good people?

When you think about bad things happening to good people, what you're really asking is, "Is there justice in the world?"

The better societies in the world make earnest attempts toward justice, but it is only partial at best. Every man and woman has a role in justice, but everyone falls short, sometimes dreadfully short. And so the pain of injustice continues.

The real damage of sin is that the consequences don't just affect the person who sinned—all those within that person's jurisdiction are affected.

But not forever. God, who is unfailingly just, can be trusted to bring final justice to every soul. David discovered that the two most foundational facets of God's character are His unconditional love and His unbeatable power (see Psalm 62:11–12). Is that reality anchored in your soul yet? Can you trust God when justice is delayed?

The only antidote for sin is the cross of Jesus—and the power of that antidote transcends, unbelievably, the power of sin and suffering. The mission of Jesus—and the church—is to bring the life-giving, sin-busting, pain-transforming grace of God to a world desperate for relief.

I had almost lost my faith because . . . I saw wicked people doing well . . . I tried to understand all this, but it was too hard for me to see until I went to the Temple of God. Then I understood what will happen to them.
Psalm 73:2–3, 16–17 NCV

Living to the Hilt

JIM AND ELISABETH ELLIOT
Fearless Missionaries

Wherever you are, be all there. Live to the hilt every situation you believe to be the will of God.

Jim Elliot

They met at Wheaton College. Two young, idealistic warriors, ready to take on the world for God. And so they did.

Bucking pressures to settle down to a more normal life of ministry in America, they waited and prayed until they were sure they had heard the will of God for their lives. South America. The unreached tribes. "Why should some hear twice," Jim declared, "when others have not heard [the gospel] once?" Their passion set its sights upon the Auca tribe of natives—a fierce, primitive group in the jungles of Ecuador.

Throughout the fall of 1955, their team of missionaries dropped gifts from a plane, attempting to assuage the hostility of the tribe that had recently killed several employees of Shell Oil. In January 1956, five men landed their little plane on a riverbank and made several friendly contacts. Yet only two days later, Jim and his friends were all speared and hacked to death by Auca warriors.

What a loss. What an unspeakable tragedy. Jim and Betty had been married only a little over two years. They had a baby girl named Valerie. How could this be, in any sense, a successful spiritual engagement?

But spiritual warfare doesn't follow the rules and assumptions of this world and its system. Personal sacrifice, just as in Jesus' case, releases spiritual power. That power carried Elisabeth Elliot forward in outreach to the Aucas over the next few years, an outreach that resulted in the entire tribe being reached with the good news. Further, that power has been a catalyst for releasing thousands of young men and women throughout the world with a missionary vision. Even *Life* magazine featured a ten-page article on Jim and Betty's compelling vision, the sacrifice made, and the Kingdom results.

Satan's central task and desire is to prevent God from being glorified. Whenever God is not glorified in a person's life, in a church, in a city, or in the world as a whole, Satan has to that degree accomplished his objective . . . Satan's primary objective is to prevent God from being glorified by keeping lost people from being saved . . . Satan's secondary objective is to make human beings and human society as miserable as possible in this present life.

Peter Wagner

wisdom from the now

Prayer is not the means
to an end. In so many
ways, it is the end itself.

Beth Moore

Intimacy in Action

There are many kinds of prayer—petitioning prayer, silent prayer, intercessory prayer, thanksgiving prayer, warfare prayer, even what some call "listening prayer" and "soaking prayer." But at its heart, prayer is nothing more or less than opening up your heart to Jesus.

Prayer is the language of intimacy, the channel of intimacy, and the evidence of intimacy. Whether it's a quick breath at a stoplight, an eloquent benediction in church, or a long discussion in the solitude of your room, prayer is connection. Prayer is alignment. Prayer is transparency.

Prayer is perhaps the greatest asset in the spiritual life. You don't have to go to a temple; you don't have to wait for a certain time of day and kneel to the east; you don't even have to speak. One honest thought heavenward, and the channel is open. It's your high-speed, always-on connection with an audience of One.

Prayer

the buzz

Every Christ-follower is on a road to increasing maturity and intimacy in their spiritual life. Prayer is perhaps the best barometer of that process.

Early faith is often characterized by a bit of intimidation regarding prayer—an uncertain desire to "get it right" or to pray intelligently. But prayer, like everything else in the Christian life, is not about performance. God doesn't care what words you use, how long or how loud you pray. He is intent upon your heart. Some of His favorite prayers are contained in one line, or even in one word: "Help!" "Jesus." "Show me, Father." "I love You."

The moment we get tired in the waiting, God's Spirit is right alongside helping us along. If we don't know how or what to pray, it doesn't matter. He does our praying in and for us, making prayer out of our wordless sighs, our aching groans.

Romans 8:26 MSG

As faith develops, you usually become comfortable conversing with God. God is discovered to be that best friend whom you can talk to about absolutely anything. You become secure, knowing that you can't shock God. He knows it all anyway; but He loves to hear it from you personally. He loves the trust that pervades such honesty.

As trust grows, you come to realize that every circumstance in life is an invitation into greater intimacy with God. Sin, for instance. While the initial result of sin is separation from that free sense of God's nearness, maturity and experience teach you that repentance is instant restoration of that precious fellowship. And the long-term result is greater intimacy.

Difficult circumstances. Difficult people. Need for direction. Need for courage. All these are invitations to intimacy, and this intimacy comes through the vehicle of prayer.

Spiritual maturity, however, involves a new dynamic in prayer. Prayer gradually ceases to be an activity as much as it becomes part of the fabric of life itself. It's as if you no longer have to go to the peephole in heaven's door in order to get a glimpse of the Father's heart or will. Instead, the door itself gradually wears thin and becomes translucent. The light of God's Kingdom begins to gently radiate upon you throughout the day, constantly warming you with Kingdom revelation and Kingdom inspiration.

> As trust grows, you come to realize that every circumstance in life is an invitation into greater intimacy with God.

This is what Paul was getting at when he invited you to "rejoice always, pray without ceasing, in everything give thanks" (1 Thessalonians 5:16–18 NKJV). His desire was for your attention to continuously be upon God and His purposes in your every activity; prayer then describes, not a posture of head bowed and eyes closed, but the way you posture your entire life. And while times will remain that are fully devoted to communing with God, there will be an increasing sense of that fellowship where heaven pervades the entirety of your work and play, your relationships and occupations. This is the intimacy that surrounds the New Rebellion.

the insight

The most famous Christian prayer of all time is commonly known as the Lord's Prayer. With intimate warmth and strategic precision, Jesus demonstrated to His disciples the mentality for Kingdom warriors. Each facet of this brief prayer is a request for alignment with the Father's Kingdom purposes on planet Earth. It is truly a timeless prayer and an essential tool for God's rebels today.

> With intimate warmth and strategic precision, Jesus demonstrated to His disciples the mentality for Kingdom warriors.
>
>

Jesus taught His disciples this prayer as part of a larger unveiling of His Kingdom vision in Matthew 5–7. Each component contains Jesus' desire to transform His friends and followers with a brand-new culture. The Beatitudes were a collection of essential Kingdom values. The salt-and-light imagery communicated Kingdom mission. The "you've heard it said" statements brought Kingdom perspectives to the Old Testament Law.

And then Jesus came to the subject of prayer. Prayer is a matter of coming into alignment with the sum total of God's Kingdom—a matter of joining with Jesus' passion for the world God created.

Our Father in heaven, hallowed be Your name (Matthew 6:9 NKJV). This is Jesus' declaration of the source of all Kingdom activity: the Father. As you pray, begin by worshiping the Source of your life and the Author of your mission.

Your kingdom come. Your will be done on earth as it is in heaven (verse 10). This is your chance to align yourself with Jesus' purpose and your purpose—to facilitate God's will in your world. This is your intercession for God to show Himself on the earth through all His representatives.

Give us this day our daily bread (verse 11). This portion of the prayer runs in the face of the world's fearful, self-sourced pursuits of provision. This declaration ushers you into the freedom of knowing God's personal commitment to your needs.

And forgive us our debts, as we forgive our debtors (verse 12). This humble heart cry aligns you with the redemptive core of the Kingdom, your instant access to forgiveness. It also highlights the partnership God is looking for—that you would be an avenue of His lavish forgiveness to others.

And do not lead us into temptation, but deliver us from the evil one. For Yours is the kingdom and the power and the glory forever. Amen (verse 13). This petition recognizes the kingdom clash present and definitively aligns you with God's side, with His authority and lordship. You will have no other master!

Prayer

the point

The intimacy of prayer establishes and reinforces your loyalty and love for the one true God. It anchors you to the spiritual fabric of your identity and vision in the world and trumpets your heavenly ownership to the entire spiritual world. No one else will possess your deepest affections. Prayer is the jersey that declares, "I'm with Him and no one else!" Prayer is the great privilege of all sons and daughters of the Kingdom.

the talk

Prayer lays hold of God's plan and becomes the link between His will and its accomplishment on earth. Amazing things happen, and we are given the privilege of being the channels of the Holy Spirit's prayer.

ELISABETH ELLIOT

Our Lord continually spoke of prayer as a means of obtaining what we desire, and . . . seeks in every possible way to awaken in us the confident expectation of an answer.

ANDREW MURRAY

Prayer is not conquering God's reluctance, but taking hold of God's willingness.

PHILLIPS BROOKS

Work, work, from morning until late at night. In fact, I have so much to do that I shall have to spend the first three hours in prayer.

MARTIN LUTHER

the word

When you pray, don't be like the hypocrites. They love to stand in the synagogues and on the street corners and pray so people will see them. I tell you the truth, they already have their full reward.

Matthew 6:5 NCV

Always be joyful. Pray continually, and give thanks whatever happens. That is what God wants for you in Christ Jesus.

1 Thessalonians 5:16–18 NCV

If two of you on earth agree about anything you ask for, it will be done for you by my Father in heaven. For where two or three come together in my name, there am I with them.

Matthew 18:19–20 NIV

Jesus was matter-of-fact: "Yes—and if you embrace this kingdom life and don't doubt God, you'll not only do minor feats like I did to the fig tree, but also triumph over huge obstacles."

Matthew 21:21 MSG

Then He spoke a parable to them, that men always ought to pray and not lose heart, . . . "Shall God not avenge His own elect who cry out day and night to Him, though He bears long with them?"

Luke 18:1, 7 NKJV

Is anyone among you suffering? Let him pray. Is anyone cheerful? Let him sing psalms. Is anyone among you sick? Let him call for the elders of the church, and let them pray over him, anointing him with oil in the name of the Lord. And the prayer of faith will save the sick, and the Lord will raise him up . . . The effective, fervent prayer of a righteous man avails much.

James 5:13–16 NKJV

Prayer

189

the prayer tools

Read it . . .

Crafted Prayer
Graham Cooke
Praying back to God the things He has revealed.

Make Me Like Jesus
Michael Phillips
The courage to pray dangerously.

The Ministry of Intercessory Prayer
Andrew Murray
Murray's most unusual and most practical devotional book.

Prayer
Richard Foster
Simple guide to the mystery that is prayer.

The Prayer of Jabez
Bruce Wilkerson
Insightful look at 1 Chronicles 4:10.

The Prayer-Shaped Disciple
Dan R. Crawford
Become a prayer warrior.

Praying God's Word
Beth Moore
Scriptural authority over fourteen strongholds.

Primary Purpose
Ted Haggard
Changing the spiritual climate of your city.

Surf it . . .

www.cptryon.org
A virtual house of prayer with morning and evening readings.

www.sacredspace.ie/livingspace
Reflections on daily readings through the Scriptures.

www.sloppynoodle.com
Hip teen community with devotions, music, prayer, and so forth.

Hear it . . .

Awakening, Mali

Blaze, Code of Ethics

Born Again Remixes, Various

How Great Is Our God, Passion

In Christ Alone, Margaret BeckerJill

Phillips, Jill Phillips

The Prayer That Changes Everything, Stormie Omartian

Do it . . .

Pray accurately for the countries of the world, www.operationworld.com.

Retrace an ancient prayer labyrinth, web.ukonline.co.uk/paradigm/index.htm.

The Top Ten Steps to Connecting in Prayer

10 Inward—reflect, breathe, prepare.

9 Noise—declutter anxious and distracting thoughts.

8 Let go—inhale the nearness of God, exhale hindrances.

7 Hurts—acknowledge and confess your brokenness.

6 Distractions—focus thought and life upon your Source.

5 Holy space—be, receive from your heavenly Father.

4 Outward—freely you have received, freely give.

3 Self—savor the gift of God that is you.

2 Planet—feel the passion of the Creator for His cosmos.

1 Others—call forth the purposes of God in your relationships.

The Question

Do your times of doubt invite you into the pursuit of God or distance you from Him?

Every Christ-follower has moments—sometimes extended moments—where your confidence in God is shaken and you doubt things that you previously had confidence in. This is not unusual. It is sometimes the result of adopting perspectives on God and His ways from other people—perspectives that you have not worked out in your own personal journey. Even if they are true, they are bound to be tested in your own experience so that they can be earned and owned in your own soul.

At other times, doubt surfaces because of disappointment with the choices or processes of God in your life. Perhaps something bad happens to someone you love. Or you enter a season of waiting where God is proving your character instead of giving you the things you expect and want. Suddenly, your trust is shaken, and you wonder if you really know this God after all or if He is truly good.

The truth is that, although you have some knowledge of God, you know only a fraction of what is there in the heart of God. And He uses these times of disorientation and disillusionment to invite you deeper into the secret place for the truest privilege of knowing Him more. This is the unlikely gift that is available during times of doubt.

Doubt is a fork in the road: Will you trust Him and press in to explore His ways more fully, or will you pull back in attempted self-preservation and begin to distance yourself from the Source of all meaning and all goodness? Those who push through disappointment and choose trust break through into new places in God. They step over the hurdle and find truer intimacy, greater spiritual authority, and deeper destiny. Prayer becomes more authentic, more real.

> Those who push through disappointment and choose trust break through into new places in God.

This sense of cooperation with God in little things is what so astonishes me, for I never have felt it this way before . . . My part is to live this hour in continuous inner conversation with God and in perfect responsiveness to his will. To make this hour gloriously rich. This seems to be all I need think about.
Frank Laubach

Reaching a New Generation in Paris

FRANK AND DAWN WILDER

Prayer Warriors

Countless people pray far more than they know. Often they have such a "stained-glass" image of prayer that they fail to recognize what they are experiencing as prayer and so condemn themselves for not praying.

Richard Foster

They served passionately and faithfully as youth pastors for years, but they knew they were made for more. For spiritual conquest. For community. For leading a team to take on impossible tasks—like planting a thriving international church in Paris, France. Paris has been called a graveyard for churches, but for Frank and Dawn, it was perfect.

Here are some of Frank's candid thoughts on prayer:

How has your praying changed since moving to Paris?

I was mentored in a very structured approach to prayer. And although that's fine, it didn't really have life for me. Now I find myself praying organically throughout the day—just stopping as needs arise and seeing prayer punctuate my life. I try to discern what God is speaking and then mirror that back in prayer.

How does prayer affect your church-planting team?

We get together every Tuesday morning, and it's mostly about connecting with God. It's a time of encouragement and intercession. What's amazing is the answers that we're seeing to our prayers—and that makes the team excited to come and get together every week. Because it's like . . . this is working!

How aware are you of spiritual warfare in Paris?

Extremely aware. We see a real spiritual haze that hangs over Paris. It takes a very intentional effort to break through it. And when you haven't broken through, it's sort of like you're under water, and everything is harder than in America.

So when you do pray intentionally, is it fairly easy to punch through that haze and experience God's presence?

It is when we're in community. It has just been crucial for us to have those kinds of friends that we can be totally transparent with, and we know they'll go to bat for us. I truly believe that prayer is the key to breaking the spiritual haze over Paris.

wisdom from the now

Shine.
Make 'em wonder what you've got.
Make 'em wish that they were not
on the outside looking bored.
Steve Taylor, Newsboys

Shine

Every man or woman who sets his or her heart to follow Jesus is a full-time, career minister of the Kingdom of God. This is the New Rebellion call. This is your identity. At the core of your being, this is who you are and who you are meant to be.

But that's not all you are. You have a totally distinct, one-of-a-kind collection of abilities and passions that are meant to become the pipeline through which you express and live out your Kingdom call. The structure that channels your personal gifts toward Kingdom purpose is your career. Your career is not defined by your school grades, your salary aspirations, or by mere opportunity. Your career is a custom-crafted calling from God to serve Him and His designs in the world through a particular occupation.

Career

the buzz

As God releases you into a career, or refines the one you have, it is vital to view your career with a set of Kingdom "glasses" so that you can see your work the same way He does. As you begin to look with His perspective, consider these three Kingdom elements: partnership, passion, and priorities.

Kingdom partnership. When God placed Adam and Eve into the brand-new, perfect world He had created, He could have made the garden maintenance-free. He could have said, "Hey, Adam, don't worry about the gardening bit; I've got that covered." Instead, He invited Adam and Even to partner with Him in the shaping and tending of that paradise. He invited Adam to participate with Him in the creative process of naming the animals. And He invited Adam and Eve to share His own authority by ruling the world. God is all about partnership.

In all the work you are doing, work the best you can. Work as if you were doing it for the Lord, not for people. Remember that you will receive your reward from the Lord, which he promised to his people. You are serving the Lord Christ.
Colossians 3:23–24 NCV

When you wake up Monday morning and head into work, you need to see yourself as a partner with God, shaping and tending the environment He has entrusted to you—whether that environment is running an international corporation, running a self-employed business, running electrical wire, or running a home. You are not there by accident. You and God have the opportunity to build the "garden" of His Kingdom every day of your life.

Kingdom passion. God has given you dreams and motivations for a reason. Quite likely, you have not tapped out your dreams yet. Perhaps your place of employment feels like a far cry from your true passion in life; it need not be. Even as you reach for something more aligned with your destiny, you can serve the interests of heaven right where you are. Your passion for God and His ways makes you a potent force for righteousness in every relationship and every task, no matter how menial.

When you wake up Monday morning and head into work, you need to see yourself as a partner with God, shaping and tending the environment He has entrusted to you.

Kingdom priorities. Finally, it is essential that, regardless of the requirements of your job, you bring the priorities of the Kingdom into that world. You cannot be passive and allow the values of the corporate culture to define you; you must define it. You and you alone are responsible to set the boundaries and conditions under which you will work.

Your hours, your travel, your ethics, your time for family and church—the buck stops with you. No one can force you to be who you are not. And no one can stop you from being who you are, bringing the life of God into every situation, every task. Your career is by design.

Career

the insight

You may remember that Paul, the great church planter, had another career as well. He was a tentmaker (see Acts 18:3). And while this fact finds only passing reference in the many books of the Bible that refer to Paul's ministry, there are some intriguing insights buried there.

> Your career should be true to your inner wiring, your set of gifts and abilities, your passions. Otherwise, it's just a job.

Was Paul's "secular" career purely pragmatic—just the quickest, easiest way to support his "spiritual" career? Or did the secular even exist for Paul? Could it be that every occupation was simply an avenue for Paul's Kingdom calling, whether building a tent or building a church? That both "careers" were true to the divine destiny upon Paul's life? There are several good reasons to believe that this is true.

First, it's important to notice that both tentmaking and church-planting flowed out of Paul's gifting, out of that combination of natural and spiritual abilities that defined Paul's soul. He was a builder, pure and simple (see 1 Corinthians 3:10). Paul had unique vision and insight, as well as specific strategies for bringing those visions to reality. So whether he was designing the layout and structure to support a tent or designing the layout and structure to support a local church, Paul was tapping into his God-given calling in the world to do it.

This is huge as it applies to you and your career. Your career should be true to your inner wiring, your set of gifts and abilities, your passions.

Otherwise, it's just a job. And no one should work "just a job" for any longer than necessary.

The other thing that emerged in Paul's dual career track was that tentmaking, though it served his practical need for financial support, didn't end there. It was completely a vehicle for Kingdom ministry. His natural skill in making tents led him into a strategic relationship with Priscilla and Aquila in Corinth; because they were both tentmakers, they worked together in the market as well as the church.

God always has a Kingdom purpose behind your career, and it's your job to pay attention, see it, and then live in it. Can you see God's purposes in your occupation? Can you see how His inner design of your soul has prepared you for your role in today's marketplace as well as your role in today's church? This is essential to understand in order to live out your part in the New Rebellion.

Career

the point

If you know that your career is not all that God has prepared you for, don't be discouraged. Begin to pray, and expect God to open up divine opportunities for Kingdom alignment within your work world. You are meant to be a world-changer, and God is going to work that out in your life through both your career and ministry. He wants to give you a Kingdom mentality that brings tremendous purpose to everything you do, no matter where you are.

the talk

We serve God by serving others. The world defines greatness in terms of power, possessions, prestige, and position. If you can demand service from others, you've arrived. In our self-serving culture with its me-first mentality, acting like a servant is not a popular concept.

RICK WARREN

Today, Christians reluctantly work in the secular world. I want them to welcome opportunities to move in the world . . . it's about being a witness by living out your Christian life on a daily basis.

JOHN FISCHER

Whoever it is calling us is calling us by our true name. Whispering to us a secret. Telling us who we are. And showing us what we will be doing with our lives if only we have the eyes to see, the ears to hear, and the faith to follow.

KEN GIRE

the word

Jesus said to them, "My food is to do the will of Him who sent Me, and to finish His work."

John 4:34 NKJV

If people build on that foundation, using gold, silver, jewels, wood, grass, or straw, their work will be clearly seen, because the Day of Judgment will make it visible. That Day will appear with fire, and the fire will test everyone's work to show what sort of work it was.

1 Corinthians 3:12–13 NCV

God is able to make all grace abound toward you, that you, always having all sufficiency in all things, may have an abundance for every good work.

2 Corinthians 9:8 NKJV

All who heard Him were astonished at His understanding and answers. So when they saw Him, they were amazed; and His mother said to Him, "Son, why have You done this to us? Look, Your father and I have sought you anxiously." And He said to them, "Why did you seek Me? Did you not know that I must be about My Father's business?"

Luke 2:47–49 NKJV

I have a greater witness than John's; for the works which the Father has given Me to finish—the very works that I do—bear witness of Me, that the Father has sent Me.

John 5:36 NKJV

Jesus traveled through all the towns and villages, teaching in their synagogues, preaching the Good News about the kingdom, and healing all kinds of diseases and sicknesses. When he saw the crowds, he felt sorry for them because they were hurting and helpless, like sheep without a shepherd. Jesus said to his followers, "There are many people to harvest but only a few workers to help harvest them. Pray to the Lord, who owns the harvest, that he will send more workers to gather his harvest."

Matthew 9:35–38 NCV

Career

the career tools

Read it . . .

The Balanced Life
Alan Loy McGinnis
Achieving success in work and love.

Business by the Book
Larry Burkett
Biblical principles for conducting business.

Courage and Calling
Gordon Smith
Embracing your God-given potential.

Five Smooth Stones for Pastoral Work
Eugene H. Peterson
Tools for the work of ministry.

God at Work
Gene Edward Veith
Your Christian vocation in all of life.

It's Easier to Succeed Than to Fail
S. Truett Cathy
The story of one Christian pioneer in the business world.

The Marketplace Annotated Bibliography
P. Hammond, R. P. Stevens, and T. Svanoe
A Christian guide to books on work, business, and vocation.

Surf it . . .

www.christianet.com/christianjobs
Search job postings for Christians.

www.christianworkplace.com
Support for Christians in work and ministry.

www.cwahm.com
Resources and encouragement for work-at-home moms and dads.

www.ivmdl.org/weblinks.cfm
Resources for marketplace ministries.

Hear it . . .

God He Reigns, Hillsongs

Hiding Places, Selah

History, Matthew West

Lackluster, Aaron Sprinkle

Not to Us, Chris Tomlin

The Noise Inside, Adam Watts

Trusting the Angels, Jason Upton

Do it . . .

Women on the Frontlines conference,
www.encountersnetwork.com/conferences.

Work personality profile,
www.christianet.com/cgi-bin/personalitytests.cgi?mode=work.

TOP TEN

The Top Ten Tools for Discerning the Will of God

10 Prayer—bring your concerns and confusion to Him.

9 Listening—wait for the responses from His heart.

8 Community—hear God's perspectives from those who know you best.

7 Counsel—receive revelation from your spiritual authorities.

6 Scriptures—look for God's direction from His revelation.

5 Passion—recognize the deep longings God has planted within you.

4 Gifting—release the unique abilities God placed within you.

3 Opportunity—consider the natural doors God opens supernaturally.

2 Joy—welcome the Spirit's confirming presence upon right choices.

1 Confirmation—find where the above tools converge.

The Question

Is your career an extension of your ministry or just a job?

There are two questions to ask in regard to your work. First, does your current career provide an outlet for your spiritual gifts and ministry calling? Do you, like Paul, have the assurance that you are strategically positioned for Kingdom impact in the work world? If you do, fantastic! If you don't, then you need to begin searching for another career or another placement that will allow you to be true to God's design. It may take time, but you cannot afford to throw away your destiny.

Second, whether you are in your current career short-term or long-term, the question is this: How can you be a conduit for Jesus' prayer—"Your kingdom come. Your will be done"—in that place right now? How can you express your spiritual gifts in that place? How can life demonstrate the reality of God's presence among your coworkers? How can you serve them and love them with Kingdom passion in practical ways?

Let's go a step further: Are you the same person at work that you are at church? Or do you put on a different persona in those two settings? It may not be your core character that changes; it may be your language. It may be your humor. It may be your priorities. And this goes both ways—you may live more authentically at work than at church. Or maybe it's the other direction, and you are more true to your spiritual self at church than at work. This inner dissonance will work against your Kingdom effectiveness and truncate your calling.

> **I**nner dissonance will work against your Kingdom effectiveness and truncate your calling.

God has grace for you to be true to God's unique design in every location. Where you don't have to pretend to be either more spiritual or less than you actually are. Reach for it.

Keep moving towards work that releases your true purpose; don't become complacent with something that pays the bills but doesn't satisfy . . . God plants desires within us for a reason and calls us to pursue the divine partnership across challenge and risk. It may take months, years, or decades to obtain that true fit . . . but it is worth the journey. Don't settle.
Jerome Daley

A Passion to Change the World

WILLIAM WILBERFORCE
1759–1833

The voice we should listen to most as we choose vocation is the voice that we might think we should listen to least, and that is the voice of our own gladness. What can we do that leaves us with the strongest sense of sailing true north and of peace, which is much of what gladness is?

Frederick Buechner

William Wilberforce was born into a life of privilege as the son of a rich merchant. Having great vision for a career in politics, he entered the House of Commons at the age of twenty-one, and four years later won an important post, partly because the prime minister was his best friend from Cambridge.

Shortly afterward, Wilberforce entered deep discussion on the subject of faith with Isaac Milner, his former schoolmaster. The result of their study and dialogue was a deep, life-altering conversion to Christ. This brought great joy to his soul but inner conflict to his role in politics. In fact, he would have abandoned Parliament altogether except for the influence of his friend John Newton, a former slave trader (and well-known hymn writer) who convinced him that God had a vital purpose for him in the political arena.

Already, voices were being raised, particularly among the Quakers, against the economically thriving slave trade, but Parliament wasn't inclined to tackle such a thorny issue. At that point, Wilberforce was seized by a passion for the great task of bringing slavery to its knees, and he introduced the first bill for abolition.

The opposition fought fiercely, both politically and personally. Wilberforce endured relentless threats and attacks, but they only fueled his commitment. The stress of the conflict did, however, break down his health, and he was forced to withdraw for a season until he recovered. By that time, England was caught up in war with France, and the nation's attention was diverted. But by 1806, a new prime minister emerged, and opportunity was suddenly upon them.

After more than twenty years of influence, Wilberforce finally saw the House of Commons abolish the trade February 23, 1807. Yet it would take another twenty-six years, just days before his death in 1833, before Parliament would bring emancipation to all slaves in the British kingdom. Wilbur's calling and career were then complete.

wisdom from the past

Few people articulate a redemptive
message using relational terms.
We believe in logic, science, lists,
and formulas. God doesn't
use any of those.

Donald Miller

Supernaturally Natural

The gospel of Jesus Christ is always relevant to the world; Christians, however, aren't always relevant. Why is that? And what does relevance really look like today?

Your life bears a message, a message of hope and redemption. But before people in your world encounter your message, they encounter you. And who you are as a person—both inside and out—colors the message you bring. On the inside, you have God's values, and on the outside, you have cultural forms and fashions that either make those values approachable or not.

The call to the New Rebellion is to make God's good news accessible—to bring hope within reach for all those who desire the message of life. This is relevance, and relevance is found where both God and people get real. Where the church is supernaturally natural.

Relevance

the buzz

The essence of God's good news is simple. God invites men and women to embrace a heavenly King, to discover their true identity as children of the Kingdom, and to in turn invite others into the Kingdom community. However, God's people often run the risk of disconnecting from the rest of the world, of creating a vast and unnecessary gulf that prevents seekers from finding Christ. So the question is this: How much of your personal culture—the way you act, talk, dress—is genuinely molded by heaven and how much is merely adopted from others?

God's culture is the expression of heaven's values. Those values are essential to the Kingdom message and cannot be compromised. It's God's opinion that needs to shape the way you behave, the music you listen to, the shows you watch, and the things you're passionate about. And some parts of God's opinion are genuinely offensive to the human heart—the truths that you are not self-sufficient, that you need a Savior, that you were never meant to rule your own life. These are legitimate "obstacles" that the world around you must cross in order to access God's Kingdom.

I didn't take on their way of life. I kept my bearings in Christ—but I entered their world and tried to experience things from their point of view.

1 Corinthians 9:22 MSG

Yet it has been the pattern of traditions and denominations within the church to clothe themselves with many layers of nonessential cultural garb and so create a Christian subculture. When this happens, Christians add a host of additional obstacles to the gospel—"Christian" lingo, insider behavior, and so forth. Where these nonessential elements of the Christian community are out of sync with contemporary culture, they cease to be relevant.

Does this mean that the mission of Christians is simply to bring its language, dress, and music into alignment with the world in order to be relevant again? Not quite. The issue of making the gospel relevant is simple in content but a bit less simple in outworking. It's a matter of becoming real and becoming supernatural.

How much of your personal culture—the way you act, talk, dress—is genuinely molded by heaven and how much is merely adopted from others?

Spiritual seekers today, perhaps now more than ever, are hungry for those two things. They have no appetite for pretension or religious show, and they yearn for authenticity and realness regarding the human condition. They want to know that you are a genuine seeker yourself on a spiritual journey that is not always easy or pretty.

That's essential, but it's not enough in itself. God has to show up! There must be something about the followers of Christ that is beyond natural explanation; there must be evidence of the supernatural workings of God in the midst of God's people. These are the fundamental matters of relevance. Once these essentials are in place, then you can work with the more pragmatic issues of style and communication.

Relevance

the insight

Jesus was the best example of being real and supernatural. In one sense, those two qualities defined His essence: He was both fully human and fully divine. If either quality were not completely present in Him, He could not have been a Savior. Now, as Christ-followers, you carry forward the same mission—to live as He lived. You, too, must be fully human—never covering up your frailties or playing a religious masquerade—and at the same time release God's Spirit within you.

> When Jesus encountered Mary, His heart broke; feeling keenly the weight of everyone's pain, He wept long and hard.

Consider the account of Jesus raising Lazarus from the dead. Lazarus and his two sisters were probably Jesus' closest friends outside Peter, James, and John. Jesus received the word that "the one you love" was sick (John 11:3 NCV). Evidently, the vibrant realness of Jesus' love for Lazarus had a very demonstrative history to it, so much so that the phrase "the one you love" signified him and no other. This is evidence of a transparent emotional life!

Jesus' response to the message was completely supernatural. He saw what His Father was doing, and brought Himself into complete partnership with it: God wanted to raise Lazarus from the dead for His glory. Okay, got it!

When Jesus showed up in Bethany at their house a number of days later, Lazarus was, of course, dead, and his sisters, Mary and Martha, were lost in their grief. Running up to Jesus, Martha was brutally honest and yet stunningly hopeful: "Lord, if You had been here, my brother would not have died. But even now I know that whatever You ask of God, God will give You" (verses 21–22 NKJV). Jesus' response revealed both His transparency and His authority as He comforted her: "Martha, I am the source of life, both for Lazarus and for you! All who trust me will live, even though they die. If you will live in my life, you will never really die. Does this make sense to you?" (verses 25–26, loosely paraphrased).

When Jesus encountered Mary, His heart broke; feeling keenly the weight of everyone's pain, He wept long and hard. At that moment, He wasn't trying to be God the transcendent Lord of the universe; He was just being real. He connected. But then within minutes He brought the full measure of His supernatural authority to bear on those relationships and called Lazarus up out of his tomb and back into life.

Relevance

the point

As God empowers you to live supernaturally natural, the Kingdom life within you will be relevant to every person you encounter, just as it was for Jesus. When people observe your transparency and know you're not pretending to be something you're not, and when they observe God's presence flowing through you and bringing supernatural impact in your world, then you have made God's good news relevant on planet Earth. You have both connected with the world and offered it a saving hope.

the talk

Our failure to impact contemporary culture is not because we have not been relevant enough, but because we have not been real enough.

SALLY MORGENTHALER

The pursuit of cultural relevance and trendy ways of exhibiting the gospel will be just as impotent and people-consuming as any other methodology. We want the fullness of God. Only his presence is relevant to every issue. Only he can touch people and bring radical change.

GRAHAM COOKE

The test of the vitality of a religion is to be seen in its effect on the culture.

ELTON TRUEBLOOD

The average Christian has no non-Christian friends after he has known the Lord for two years.

JOE ALDRICH

the word

Jesus Christ is the same yesterday, today, and forever.

Hebrews 13:8 NKJV

You are the salt of the earth; but if the salt loses its flavor, how shall it be seasoned? It is then good for nothing but to be thrown out and trampled underfoot by men.

Matthew 5:13 NKJV

I am free and belong to no one. But I make myself a slave to all people to win as many as I can. To the Jews I became like a Jew to win the Jews. I myself am not ruled by the law. But to those who are ruled by the law I became like a person who is ruled by the law. I did this to win those who are ruled by the law. To those who are without the law I became like a person who is without the law. I did this to win those people who are without the law. (But really, I am not without God's law—I am ruled by Christ's law.) . . . I have become all things to all people so I could save some of them in any way possible.

1 Corinthians 9:19–22 NCV

Paul stood before the meeting of the Areopagus and said, "People of Athens . . . as I was going through your city, I saw . . . an altar that had these words written on it: TO A GOD WHO IS NOT KNOWN. You worship a god that you don't know, and this is the God I am telling you about!"

Acts 17:22–23 NCV

I am not asking you to take them out of the world but to keep them safe from the Evil One. They don't belong to the world, just as I don't belong to the world. Make them ready for your service through your truth; your teaching is truth. I have sent them into the world, just as you sent me into the world.

John 17:15–18 NCV

Relevance

217

the relevance tools

Read it . . .

Becoming Real
Stephen James
Stop pretending and be the authentic you.

The Gospel Reloaded
Chris Seay and Greg Garrett
Exploring spirituality and faith in The Matrix.

The Irrelevance and Relevance of the Christian Message
Paul Tillich
Biblical answers to existential questions.

The Journey Towards Relevance
Kary Oberbrunner
Simple steps for transforming your world.

Making Sense of Church
Spencer Burke and Colleen Pepper
Eavesdropping on emerging conversations about God, community, and culture.

Prophetic Untimeliness
Os Guinness
A challenge to the idol of relevance.

Searching for God Knows What
Donald Miller
Tapping the universal desire for redemption in the world.

Surf it . . .

www.emergingwomenleaders.org
Web log for women in leadership within postmodern churches.

www.ginkworld.net
Clearinghouse for postmodern thoughts and ministries.

www.sacramentis.com
Worship consulting and postmodern perspectives from Sally Morgenthaler.

www.theooze.com/main.cfm
Multithreaded conversations on postmodern ministry.

Hear it . . .

Antiphony, Paul Oakley

King of Fools, Delirious

Lifesong, Casting Crowns

Momentum, Toby Mac

Surprising, Geraldine Latty

When Silence Falls, Tim Hughes

Do it . . .

Conferences and events on church relevance, www.emergentvillage.org.

Online magazine for culture and God, www.relevantmagazine.com.

Online magazine for faith and culture, www.sevenmagazine.org.

TOP TEN

The Top Ten Ways to Be Supernaturally Relevant

10   Filter religious jargon from your language.

9   Do not filter your authentic spirituality.

8   Be respectful of other people's convictions.

7   Do not hide your own convictions.

6   Tune in to the felt needs of your culture.

5   Do not limit your spiritual gifts to church.

4   Offer advice, not judgment.

3   Expect God to work miracles in your workplace.

2   Do not hide your struggles and failures.

1   Never move in fear; always move in love.

Your life is not your own; it belongs to God. To "be yourself" is not to just be anything you want to be. To "be yourself" is to be and do what God wants you to be and do, knowing that God created you for a mission and knows you and your mission better than you do.

Leonard Sweet

The Question

-->

Are you afraid that being relevant will lead you into compromise?

No one wants to gain an audience but somehow relinquish the message. You don't want to "become so well-adjusted to your culture that you fit into it without even thinking," as it says in Romans 12:2 (MSG). No, you want to safeguard the vital, world-changing message of the gospel but then find a way to communicate it to people as clearly and convincingly as possible.

So where's the line? And how do you know if you've crossed it?

It's a matter of walking in what Jesus called the two greatest commandments—loving God and loving others. When your heart is consumed with a pervasive passion for God, then you will be free from both legalism and license. And when your love for the people around you is free of fear, then you will never assume behavior just to fit in; your character will take the shape of what people *need* you to be, not what people *want* you to be.

In practicality, you've got to filter out all the outward behavior people have tried to marry to the gospel. Drinking, dancing, card playing, moviegoing, wearing makeup, you name it. It's astounding the behavioral control that certain facets of the church have tried to enforce that are not in Scripture. While godly behavior requires maturity, Jesus made a compelling plea in the Sermon on the Mount to replace external issues with internal. The condition of the heart is God's prime concern, according to Matthew 5.

> **W**hen your love for the people around you is free of fear, then you will never assume behavior just to fit in.

Bottom line: Major on the majors; minor on the minors. Relate to people in a way that's authentic to who you are. Let your life back up your words. Love God, allowing all you do and say to come under the scrutiny of His Spirit. Love people, respecting what they think but not being controlled by it.

Mine was not a crisis of faith in the typical sense; I never doubted God, Jesus, or the Christian faith. And yet I had a deep sense, which has actually grown deeper since, that I needed to move into a Christianity that somehow fit better with the world I lived in and not an expression reconstituted from another time.
Doug Pagitt

An Early Postmodern

SAINT CATHERINE OF SIENA
1347–1380

Man is placed above all creatures, and not beneath them, and he cannot be satisfied or content except in something greater than himself. Greater than himself there is nothing but Myself, the Eternal God. Therefore I alone can satisfy him.

From a vision to Saint Catherine, 1370

The world that Saint Catherine was born into was not unlike your own. Though it was fourteenth-century Italy, the cultural current was in huge transition between the medieval age and the rising Renaissance. Today's world is caught in an equally turbulent transition between the modern world inaugurated by the Renaissance and the emerging postmodern world. The seasons of changing mind-sets and world-views open windows of opportunity for those with Kingdom vision and passion. Catherine was such a woman.

Ignited by a vision of Jesus at the age of seven, Catherine set a course for a life of spiritual connection with God and service to people. But rather than choose the physical confinement of a convent, she instead joined the Sisters of Penitences, a Dominican order for lay ministry, where she would be free to serve the neediest of her region. She was drawn inexorably to those who suffered most painfully.

In a day when a woman's place was in the home—or tucked neatly away in a convent—Catherine rebelled against those confinements to pursue her spiritual destiny. She nursed those incurably ill with cancer or leprosy; she counseled and evangelized among prisoners condemned to die; she spread spiritual insights and advice through her writings. But as her following swelled, her critics also increased. In fact, she became the target of mounting opposition from conservative church leaders who disapproved of her activism, culminating in a Dominican tribunal on charges of heresy.

Known for her intimate mystical experiences with God, Catherine bridged the gap between heavenly passion and earthly service—more than anyone else of her time—and proved that relevance is a timeless commodity. She disregarded empty religious conventions that paralyzed others and pursued Kingdom transformation in her world. And in so doing, she bravely entered the ranks of the New Rebellion.

wisdom from the past

Getting Real

SALLY MORGENTHALER

Founder of Sacramentis.com and President of Digital Glass Productions

What we have done so often is to substitute abstractions—propositions—for the stories of God . . . If we were to re-tell the narrative of the woman anointing Jesus' feet—in our congregation's language, and accompanied by one artist's interpretation of it . . . we would probably be much more faithful to the Word.

Sally Morgenthaler

Sally was a worship leader for years before taking her probing insights into a larger ministry of worship consultation. She asks the hard questions and does what every student of church and culture should do: hold up a mirror so that the church can see itself with more honest perspective.

Author of *Worship Evangelism: Inviting Unbelievers into the Presence of God*, Morgenthaler offered a few thoughts on relevance in the following interview with Fred Peatross:

How does a congregation know when to contemporize their assemblies in order to connect with culture?

There are . . . reasons behind our change reticence that don't stand up so well, namely, anything that falls into the category of, "This is the way we've always done it." If God had said this, there would have been no Incarnation; there would have been no great hymns of the faith. It is this incarnation mentality that needs to be at the root of worship change. We are living in a different time. People speak English differently than they did even a decade ago. Artistic and musical styles have changed. To remain the same is not an option, even if we just want to keep the people we have.

Can you give us your thoughts on the worship assembly and its place as cultural outreach?

Here's how I view worship evangelism: experiencing God in the context of a church that is both spiritually and culturally engaged; worship that is whole-person, engaging all the senses and full range of emotions—the unabashed celebration of brokenness, paradox, and unanswered questions. It's about deconstructing and reconstructing tradition, about fusing the ancestral to the now.

When the epitaph is written on your ministry, what do you want it to read?

That God was able to speak and act through me, both in spite of my humanity and because of it.

wisdom from the now

I dream of a church, which does not need huge amounts of money, or rhetoric, control and manipulation, which can do without powerful and charismatic heroes, which is non-religious at heart, which can thrill people to the core, make them lose their tongues out of sheer joy and astonishment, and simply teach us The Way to live.

Wolfgang Simson

Community That Empowers

You can discover your destiny only within the context of community.

When God put you together, He gave you a set of strengths, gifts, and abilities. Along with those assets, He also gave you a set of liabilities: your own unique weaknesses, blind spots, and shortcomings. And while those things can be a source of frustration, they are actually a gift from heaven.

God built you to be dependent upon others—first upon Him and second upon other people. This means that you are absolutely dependent upon your community to come into wholeness—you need them, and they need you. This interdependence is the goal of church, your spiritual community. Community is the concept; church is the means. So whether sitting with hundreds on Sunday morning or with a handful in a small group, you can tap the brilliance of God's design.

Community & Church

1 the buzz

You do not have every asset and resource necessary to fulfill your assignment on planet Earth. For this reason, and many others, God invites you to discover the community of church and live within the freedom it brings. Not that community is always easy—people are complicated, and relationships eventually involve mess. But community is defined by people's commitment to one another and to the call of Christ and by their willingness to work through messes for your good and theirs.

The church is not an institution, although it requires certain structures. The church is not a collection of historical creeds and forms, although it is rooted in its past. What is the church? Well, it's many things, but at its heart, the church is a community of faith, a band of brothers and sisters with a common Kingdom calling that brings them together and then sends them out. Here are some practical ways that the church empowers your life.

His purpose was that through the church all the rulers and powers in the heavenly world will now know God's wisdom, which has so many forms.
Ephesians 3:10 NCV

Community stabilizes. You need your church community partly because you need an anchor when a life storm blows you sideways. Whether your storm is doubt or difficulty or disorientation, the love of your community brings enormous stability to your soul when it's rocked by circumstances.

Community interprets. People usually lack the larger perspective needed to make sense out of their own life events. Because it's so close and so personal, meaning tends to get skewed and distorted unless trusted souls walk alongside you who have the freedom to speak perspective into your life.

Community instructs. Humility is that rare and wonderful ability to receive instruction and equipping from others. You have blind spots—you know that, right? The church community has the opportunity to encourage you and also challenge you, to comfort you and also correct you. This function flows to the extent that trust and humility reside in each heart.

> At its heart, the church is a community of faith, a band of brothers and sisters with a common Kingdom calling that brings them together and then sends them out.

Community defends. Since life happens within the context of spiritual war, it is essential to know that you have people who love you surrounding you in prayer, warring against your spiritual enemies. Your community of faith, if it's doing its job, will protect you both from the enemy and from yourself. They will identify the real foe and stand with you for victory.

Community empowers. By covering your weaknesses with their strengths, by stabilizing your soul and interpreting the currents of life, your community releases you into your true destiny. They call the deposit of God out of you. They believe in you and affirm your true identity. They empower you to rebel against worldly culture and contend for Kingdom culture.

Community & Church

the insight

Among those who contended for the Kingdom were Barnabas and Paul, and one of the first places they sowed community was in the city of Antioch. The outreach there began as the result of the persecution that inflamed Jerusalem upon the martyrdom of Stephen. A handful of Christians who fled Jerusalem made their way to Antioch and found many who were receptive to the good news.

> Every Christ-follower is on a journey of spiritual formation—to be fashioned into the real man or woman God had in mind for them when He created them.

Hearing that God was moving there, the Jerusalem church sent Barnabas to Antioch to bring some apostolic direction to the newly birthed church. Acts 11 says that Barnabas "saw evidence of the grace of God" (verse 23 NIV) upon the group, which is significant. Despite the persecution in Jerusalem, this group of new believers found *stability* in the new community that God had brought together. Barnabas's presence among them sparked further outreach, and the community continued to grow.

Still, Barnabas understood that, no matter how anointed he was, he needed teamwork within the community—and so he convinced Paul to join him there where they spent the next year *instructing* the new church.

But community was not just for the church's own benefit; a healthy church will always express itself outwardly as well. Discovering a financial crisis in Judea, the Antioch church gathered a collection to *empower* the believers in that region. And even as King Herod turned up the heat of persecution throughout the area (see Acts 12), the church joined together in prayer to *defend* itself against its enemies.

But the apex of their community expressed itself a short time later. By this time, a whole leadership team had sprung out of their community, and together in worship, prayer, and fasting, God released wisdom and direction that *interpreted* His will to send Paul and Barnabas out from Antioch on their first missionary journey.

All Christ-followers are on journeys of spiritual formation—to be fashioned into the real men and women God had in mind for them when He created them. For their characters to be established and refined. For their gifts and abilities to be released purposefully. For their dreams and destiny to be fulfilled in God's Kingdom. For these things, God established the church community to be a safe place, a place authentically real and supernaturally potent, where the convergence of God's children would fit together into a body, as Paul described it. Together, and only together, can the Kingdom flow in the earth.

the point

Community is the essence of the Kingdom that God is bringing to the earth. He intends for this interdependence to empower your life and bring you into alignment with the character of Christ. And this quality of community is what we call church. Whether in large groups or small, God will stabilize you, interpret life, bring instruction, protect you, and empower your purpose through the relationships that make up your spiritual community.

the talk

A striking feature of worship in the Bible is that people gathered in what we would call "holy expectancy." They believed they would actually hear the voice of God. It was not surprising to them that the building in which they met shook with the power of God.

RICHARD FOSTER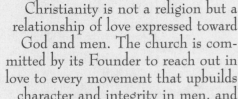

In the essentials—unity, in the nonessentials—freedom, in all things—love.

JOHN WESLEY

Christianity is not a religion but a relationship of love expressed toward God and men. The church is committed by its Founder to reach out in love to every movement that upbuilds character and integrity in men, and every gesture that aims to resolve the differences that estrange human beings from each other. The Gospel in its free course goes hand-in-hand with the cup of cold water.

SHERWOOD ELIOT WIRT

Rather than growing bigger churches, we should be concerned with growing bigger Christians.

RICH MULLINS

the word

Greater love has no one than this, than to lay down one's life for his friends.

John 15:13 NKJV

Comfort each other and edify one another, just as you also are doing.

1 Thessalonians 5:11 NKJV

This is the rock on which I will put together my church, a church so expansive with energy that not even the gates of hell will be able to keep it out.

Matthew 16:18 MSG

Be careful for yourselves and for all the people the Holy Spirit has given to you to care for. You must be like shepherds to the church of God, which he bought with the death of his own son.

Acts 20:28 NCV

They spent their time learning the apostles' teaching, sharing, breaking bread, and praying together. The apostles were doing many miracles and signs, and everyone felt great respect for God. All the believers were together and shared everything.

Acts 2:42–44 NCV

I have given these people the glory that you gave me so that they can be one, just as you and I are one. I will be in them and you will be in me so that they will be completely one. Then the world will know that you sent me and that you loved them just as much as you loved me.

John 17:22–23 NCV

Community & Church

233

the church & community tools

Read it . . .

Connecting
Larry Crabb
Building intimate healing minicommunities.

The Connecting Church
Randy Frazee
Beyond small groups to authentic community.

Creating Community
Andy Stanley and Bill Willits
Five keys to building a small group.

The Emerging Church
Dan Kimball, Rick Warren, and others
Exploring cultural changes.

God's Favorite House
Tommy Tenney
Restoring the passion of worship that invites God home.

Houses That Change the World
Wolfgang Simson
The global resurgence of house churches.

The Life-Giving Church
Ted Haggard
Values for bringing life back to church.

Reimagining Spiritual Formation
Doug Pagitt
A week in the life of an experimental church.

Surf it . . .

www.emergingchurch.org
Resources to make ancient faith relevant in today's world.

www.jesus.org.uk
How one group is doing church in the UK.

www.pastorsretreatnetwork.com
Retreat centers for people in full-time Christian pastoral ministry.

Hear it . . .

Come Together, Third Day

Just Like Heaven, Anaheim Vineyard

Lift Him Up Collection, Ron Kenoly

Look to You, Hillsong United

Redemption Songs, Jars of Clay

The Thesis, The Ambassador

World Service, Delirious

Your Kingdom Come, Andrew Mitchell

Do it . . .

Building practical community by building houses, www.habitat.org.

Christ for the Nations: Bible School and church-planting, www.cfni.org.

Conferences and events to equip, www.cookministries.com/events.

TOP TEN

The Top Ten Ways to Build Community

10 Use self-disclosure to get real.

9 Listen more than you talk.

8 Ask good questions to uncover meaning.

7 Have fun! Don't make everything overtly spiritual.

6 Use your spiritual gifts to encourage others.

5 Balance activity inward, outward, and upward.

4 Serve those outside your community as a community.

3 Share the significant issues of your past.

2 Probe one another's dreams for the future.

1 Love one another practically and consistently.

Trust, unfortunately, develops only within the context of stress and difficulty, for it is in that setting that people reveal their true selves . . . and their true place within the community . . . In these moments we discover, perhaps to our surprise, who is committed to us with a love beyond affection, who lives for our good when the cost is high.

Jerome Daley

The Question

Who are the people in your life you know would walk you through any crisis?

Everyone gets a turn at crisis. And more than once. The real question is only this: Who in your life is both capable of and willing to walk through your crises with you? In many ways, your life will be defined by the quality of people who journey alongside you.

The trouble with crises is that they don't show up on your organizer. They are unsought and unexpected. Crises come on their own terms, and when they do, the scaffold of a nurturing, supporting community is either there or it isn't. Usually, there isn't time to start building the scaffold once the foundation is rocking and stones are falling.

Jesus said that the "wise man" built his house on the rock so when the thunderstorms broke and the floodwaters rose and the hurricane winds all beat on that house, it stood securely (see Matthew

7:24). In contrast, the house built on sandy soil was absolutely destroyed in the storm. What is that securing rock? Well, it's Christ— but not just Christ; it is Christ incarnated in your community!

So the question remains: Whom will you turn to when the dark clouds come broiling in over your life? Who will stabilize you, interpret the storm, instruct you, defend you, and empower your destiny?

The answer? It will be the same community that you allow full, unfiltered access to your soul—and them to you—when everything is going great in your life.

This is the life of the Kingdom, that you are not alone.

The ones who share life meaningfully with you day in and day out are the ones who will recognize your storm and come to your aid when it hits. They can't make the storm go away, but they can commune with you throughout it, and this is the life of the Kingdom, that you are not alone. You have a Savior, and you have a saving community.

A man who has friends must himself be friendly, but there is a friend who sticks closer than a brother.
Proverbs 18:24 NKJV

Reimagining Community

DOUG PAGITT

Experimental Church-Planter

Solomon's Porch was fueled by a desire to find a new way of life with Jesus, in community with others, that honored my past and moved boldly into the future.

Doug Pagitt

inding faith at sixteen, Pagitt quickly found himself a leader in his high school's Christian group. After college came seminary and then ten years of a youth pastorate. The evangelical tradition that nurtured him laid a solid biblical foundation and a vibrant relationship with Christ. But eventually a nagging discontent emerged.

So Pagitt began to meet with a handful of other believers who shared a common vision for an uncommon faith—for new expressions to an ancient faith—and a more missional community. Calling themselves Solomon's Porch, they began to reach for a faith that would be genuinely useful in the world. Three core values motivate them:

Post older traditions, not anti or against. Within this community was a deep appreciation for the heritage of their past, even while they felt a consuming motivation to grow beyond it. So they have adopted the prefix *post* to describe their ongoing journey: post-evangelical, post-liberal, post-industrialized, and post-Protestant. After, but not against. Their passion is to "be always re-forming—always seeking to create new ways of life and new ideas about theology, service, and love."

Organic, not imitation. Pagitt's crew has an innate distaste for replicating someone else's church model. Instead, they allowed the values of their own new community to begin to give expression to their faith in ways that were genuinely organic. Incorporating the pieces of their past that had meaning and connection, they also allow a creative, innovational spirit to mold the community they are becoming.

Gatherings, not "services." Together they are reaching for an authentic means to live a shared life among the community of faith. "I didn't want to become a provider of religious goods and services, no matter how hip they were." That well-traveled philosophy breeds an inherent consumer mentality that undermines the quality of community so essential to the Kingdom of God. So, the experiment continues.

wisdom from the now

Forgiveness is the
final form of love.

Reinhold Niebuhr

The Fatal Blow to Pride

Is there anything more liberating, more compelling, more transforming than forgiveness? It's a quality that this world cannot comprehend or manufacture—it's the very breath of heaven, the aroma of life! It's what you're made for, both to receive and to give.

Because of the Kingdom power bound up in forgiveness, it is contested strongly by your spiritual enemy. Both accepting and extending forgiveness can be the most difficult things you face. Still, the Kingdom life can't be lived successfully without an ongoing revelation and operation of forgiveness.

The secret behind forgiveness's power is that it confronts—and has the ability to set you free from—your pride. If there is one thing that runs contrary to the Kingdom culture of God, it's pride: the elevation of self. Pride is your most consistent enemy in the New Rebellion. But Jesus has provided an enduring solution.

Sin & Forgiveness

the buzz

There are two dominant personality profiles, and each confronts the issue of forgiveness from a vastly different perspective than the other: mercy-driven individuals and justice-driven individuals. While both qualities are biblical, people generally fall more naturally into alignment with one or the other. You tend to respond to people either with comfort or with truth. Do you know which motivation best describes you?

When it comes to forgiveness, mercy-driven people generally find it easy to forgive others but difficult to forgive themselves—to accept forgiveness from others or from God. In contrast, justice-driven people usually accept forgiveness easily but find it difficult to forgive others. Regardless of which motivation best describes you, each can represent opposite but equal expressions of pride.

Those who are moved by mercy find it hard to receive grace because they intuitively believe, "I *should* be better than this. Don't you recognize that about me?" Those motivated by justice believe, "I *am* better than this! And you should be too." Both of those responses flow from pride—out of an elevated opinion of one's self and the desire to protect that elevated self. But pride in any form shuts down the Kingdom flow of authentic repentance and forgiveness.

If we say we have no sin, we are fooling ourselves, and the truth is not in us. But if we confess our sins, he will forgive our sins, because we can trust God to do what is right. He will cleanse us from all the wrongs we have done.

1 John 1:8–9 NCV

Psalm 85:10 brings these two extremes together in God: "Mercy and truth have met together; righteousness and peace have kissed" (NKJV). And this is the heavenly reality—both virtues find their proper, life-giving intersection in Christ. And the place that mercy and truth meet is called *grace*. Grace is the conduit for forgiveness. Grace is the vehicle where heaven invades earth with Kingdom redemption.

So what's your role in grace? Your life can become a channel for forgiveness. You can irrigate the dry, cracked lakebed of your world. Your life can dispense grace freely, bringing hope to parched people everywhere. How? Make it your mission to release people from your judgment, even if you're right. Especially if you're right.

Proverbs 19:11, written by King Solomon, illuminates, "A man's wisdom gives him patience; it is to his glory to overlook an offense" (NIV). Jesus made it a point to ask His Father numerous times to forgive people of the gravest sins, even those who nailed Him on a cross. Those who legitimately deserved the most severe justice.

> You tend to respond to people either with comfort or with truth. Do you know which motivation best describes you?

Finally, you have to be able to humbly receive the mercy and forgiveness that God lavishly pours out upon you. This truly is humility. It honors God and demonstrates His passion for amazing grace.

Sin & Forgiveness

the insight

The Christ-follower uniquely known as the "disciple Jesus loved" related this riveting drama in John 8:3–11 (NCV).

"The teachers of the law and the Pharisees brought a woman who had been caught in adultery. They forced her to stand before the people. They said to Jesus, 'Teacher, this woman was caught having sexual relations with a man who is not her husband. The law of Moses commands that we stone to death every woman who does this. What do you say we should do?'" (verses 3–5).

> Shame is the acknowledgement of guilt and, at the same time, a denial of redemption.
>
>

The Pharisees were using this question as a trap in order to have a basis for accusing Him. But Jesus bent down and started to write on the ground with His finger. When they kept on questioning Him, He straightened up and said to them, "Anyone here who has never sinned can throw the first stone at her" (verse 7).

Again He stooped down and wrote on the ground. At that, those who heard began to go away one at a time, the older ones first, until only Jesus was left with the woman who was still standing there. Jesus straightened up and asked her, "Woman, where are they? Has no one judged you guilty?" (verse 10).

"No one, sir," she said. "I also don't judge you guilty," Jesus declared. "You may go now, but don't sin anymore" (verse 11).

A number of questions beg to be answered. First, where is the man?

A woman can't commit adultery solo. And the same law that assigned the death penalty to an adulteress also commanded death for the adulterer. There was a double standard in first-century Jewish culture that winked at men's indiscretions but struck venomously at women. A standard that knew both license and judgment but not grace.

Second, what was the motivation of the Pharisees? Was it really love for Moses' law? Not hardly. Their motivation, confirmed by John's commentary, was pride. They laid their most clever trap for Jesus. Why? In order to protect their own system of religious power from the greatest threat that system had ever seen.

In characteristic discernment, Jesus ignored their power play, sidestepped their trap, and unmasked their self-righteous facade. What was the Pharisees' response? Essentially, shame. But not repentance. Shame is the acknowledgment of guilt and, at the same time, a denial of redemption. It is a piercing observation that the "older ones" slipped away first after Jesus' challenge; they knew their own need for forgiveness all too well, but they still chose to deny it.

Sin & Forgiveness

the point

The forgiveness Jesus offered that traumatized woman was a picture of true grace: a grace that cleansed her shame, covered her past, redirected her future, and empowered her with new vision. The forgiveness that flows from your life will be equally powerful. When mercy and justice meet inside your heart, you will dispense the refreshing grace of God in everything you do and say. You will empower instead of condemn.

the talk

The world can do almost anything as well as or better than the church. You need not be a Christian to build houses, feed the hungry, or heal the sick. There is only one thing the world cannot do. It cannot offer grace.

GEORGE MACDONALD

Many years ago I was driven to the conclusion that the two major causes of most emotional problems among evangelical Christians are these: the failure to understand, receive, and live out God's unconditional grace and forgiveness; and the failure to give out that unconditional love, forgiveness, and grace to other people.

DAVID SEAMONDS

I rejected the church for a time because I found so little grace there. I returned because I found grace nowhere else.

PHILIP YANCEY

the word

If we confess our sins, he will forgive our sins, because we can trust God to do what is right. He will cleanse us from all the wrongs we have done.

1 John 1:9 NCV

Get along with each other, and forgive each other. If someone does wrong to you, forgive that person because the Lord forgave you.

Colossians 3:13 NCV

Be kind to one another, tenderhearted, forgiving one another, even as God in Christ forgave you.

Ephesians 4:32 NKJV

If a fellow believer hurts you, go and tell him—work it out between the two of you.

Matthew 18:15 MSG

If he sins against you seven times in one day and says that he is sorry each time, forgive him.

Luke 17:4 NCV

Confess your trespasses to one another, and pray for one another, that you may be healed. The effective, fervent prayer of a righteous man avails much.

James 5:16 NKJV

LORD, even before I say a word, you already know it . . . Your knowledge is amazing to me; it is more than I can understand . . . God, examine me and know my heart; test me and know my nervous thoughts. See if there is any bad thing in me. Lead me on the road to everlasting life.

Psalm 139:4, 6, 23–24 NCV

Sin & Forgiveness

the sin &
forgiveness tools

Read it . . .

Broken on the Back Row
Sandi Patty
A journey through grace and
forgiveness.

Calvary Road
Roy Hession
The liberating walk of brokenness.

Embracing Forgiveness
Traci Mullins
Group study on the price of forgiveness.

The Gift of Forgiveness
Charles Stanley
How to appropriate God's grace.

The Pressure's Off
Larry Crabb
Living with passion and without
pressure.

The Root of the Righteous
A. W. Tozer
Essays on solving everyday problems.

Total Forgiveness
R. T. Kendall
The story of Joseph teaches how to
forgive those who hurt us.

What's So Amazing About Grace?
Philip Yancey
What grace does and doesn't look like.

Surf it . . .

www.brokenwalls.com
A musical reconciliation ministry to
Native Americans.

www.ethnicharvest.org
Resources for racial reconciliation.

www.forgiving.org
A campaign for forgiveness research.

Hear it . . .

Clean, Jim Robinson

Grace Like Rain, Todd Agnew

Healing Rain, Michael W. Smith

In the Company of Angels,
Caedmon's Call

Mercy in the Wilderness, Steve Camp

Mmhmm, Relient K

Restored, Jeremy Camp

Short Term Memories, Chris Rice

Do it . . .

Events for Christian healing,
www.reconciliationnetworks.org.

Resolve church conflicts,
www.resolvechurchconflict.com.

Visit the "apology room,"
www.forgivenessweb.com.

TOP TEN

The Top Ten Ways to Grow in Grace

10 Be quick to acknowledge sin and guilt.

9 Live in the confidence of your divine ownership.

8 Easily receive God's forgiveness that invites you into intimacy.

7 Stop trying to earn God's favor; you already have it.

6 Reject false guilt—it is the enemy's favorite lie.

5 Take every opportunity to overlook the failures of others.

4 Call attention to people's potential, not their faults.

3 Speak the truth in gentleness and love.

2 Don't pretend to have your life all neatly together.

1 Be quick to forgive, slow to be offended.

Grace is Christianity's best gift to the world, a spiritual nova in our midst exerting a force stronger than vengeance, stronger than racism, stronger than hate.

Philip Yancey

The Question

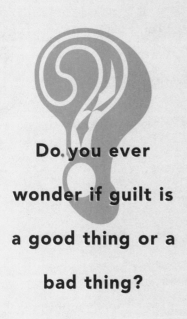

Do you ever wonder if guilt is a good thing or a bad thing?

Guilt, it seems, can lead people to places both good and bad—either to repentance and restoration or to grief and despair. So how does a holy rebel handle such a perplexing and unreliable feeling? Or, considered differently, can guilt be made a servant of the Kingdom?

First, it's essential to know that guilt is not in itself a condition of the soul; rather, it is a symptom or an indicator of a soul condition. Just as pain in your body indicates when something is wrong, so guilt is a red flag of warning that something is broken in the soul. So what does guilt warn of? It warns of the presence of sin, either real or perceived.

Guilt is a motivator to search out that sin source and deal with it. If you understand the power of God's grace demonstrated in the life and death of Jesus, then the recognition of sin is just one more invitation to intimacy. The sorrow of having disobeyed God is quickly replaced by the overwhelming affection of God that covers the sin and erases the guilt. This is surely a case in which guilt is a good thing.

So when is guilt a bad thing? There are two occasions: First, there are circumstances in which you can *feel* false guilt; in other words, your heart condemns you, but you haven't actually sinned. First John 3:19–20 assures you that you can rest in God and lay that false guilt aside. Second, guilt is a bad thing when the bearer refuses to heed its call, ignores the sin that initiates it, and either denies legitimate guilt or allows unresolved guilt to fester and poison the soul.

Just as pain in your body indicates when something is wrong, so guilt is a red flag of warning that something is broken in the soul.

What is clear is that Jesus resolves fully all sin and guilt for the New Rebellion Christ-follower. Guilt is God's tool and not to be feared.

We must develop and maintain the capacity to forgive. He who is devoid of the power to forgive is devoid of the power to love. There is some good in the worst of us and some evil in the best of us. When we discover this, we are less prone to hate our enemies.
Martin Luther King Jr.

Rescued by Grace

MARTIN LUTHER
1483–1546

Sincere forgiveness isn't colored with expectations that the other person apologize or change. Don't worry whether or not they finally understand you. Love them and release them. Life feeds back truth to people in its own way and time.

Sara Paddison

Easily the most significant figure in Protestant church history, Luther is best known for his Ninety-five Theses tacked to the door of the Wittenberg Church in 1517, and the subsequent furor when Luther renounced papal authority and in turn was excommunicated from the Catholic Church. What is frequently less known is his own personal struggle with sin and guilt that led him to a discovery of grace unprecedented in the medieval era.

Neither his years as an earnest monk nor his use of penance and the sacraments could remove Luther's sense of guilt and failure to live up to God's standard of righteousness. The more he tried to live a holy life and atone for his sins, the more oppressed he became. At the same time, he grew increasingly critical of indulgences—a corruption of the penance sacrament that promised forgiveness of sins for a price.

But it wasn't until after his theses were posted that Luther experienced the transforming breakthrough of personal conversion. Romans 1:17 opened the door of revelation for him: "The Good News shows how God makes people right with himself—that it begins and ends with faith. As the Scripture says, 'But those who are right with God will live by trusting in him'" (NCV). Suddenly the brilliance of grace thrust itself upon his tortured soul, and he understood that Christ's righteousness had become his, unlocked through a simple trusting faith.

As he began to publish his discoveries, Luther was ordered to recant, was subsequently banished from the church, and finally was declared a civil outlaw. His very life would have been taken if not for the protection of Prince Frederick of Saxony, who arranged for him to live secretly in the castle of Wartburg where he wrote for another twenty-five years before dying of natural causes. If there was ever a holy rebel, it was that man.

wisdom from the past

Success is not final, failure is not fatal: it is the courage to continue that counts.

Winston Churchill

The Risk to Reach

The New Rebellion implies a conflict. A rebel is always bucking the norm, swimming upstream, contending for a cause. This makes the quality of courage absolutely requisite. Without courage, the best of intentions will accomplish little; in fact, vision without courage will merely produce a rising tide of frustration.

Courage is more than just a willingness to engage in conflict. It's a willingness to go the distance when the vision has faded, when you're weary, when no one is there to cheer you on. Courage is an enduring commitment to be your true self when no one is looking and you're facing intimidation.

The heroes of the faith were men and women who risked great loss in order to pursue Jesus' prayer: "Your Kingdom come"! They stood out from the crowd and did what no one else was willing to do. And the world is different because of it.

Courage

the buzz

Courage is counterintuitive for most people. The urge for self-preservation pushes most souls into the mainstream where they can be carried along with maximum acceptance and minimum risk. They may not like where the mainstream is headed, but they lack the motivation to resist it or reach for something better.

When it comes to following Christ, this lack of courage is called "nominalism"—people who like the idea of being a Christian and may even go to church, but they draw back from making any personal sacrifice on behalf of God's Kingdom. Jesus cuts this group no slack with these challenging words:

According to my earnest expectation and hope that in nothing I shall be ashamed, but with all boldness, as always, so now also Christ will be magnified in my body, whether by life or by death.
Philippians 1:20 NKJV

"Not all those who say that I am their Lord will enter the kingdom of heaven. The only people who will enter the kingdom of heaven are those who do what my Father in heaven wants. On the last day many people will say to me, 'Lord, Lord, we spoke for you, and through you we forced out demons and did many miracles.' Then I will tell them clearly, 'Get away from me, you who do evil. I never knew you'" (Matthew 7:21–23 NCV).

Courage has a number of facets to it: the willingness to oppose, the willingness to be opposed, the willingness to wait, and the willingness to not give up. The first is the most obvious—the man or woman of courage faces very real fears, threats, and risks in order to contend against something evil. What is God calling you to oppose in your world? One thing to remember here is that it isn't people. Remember Paul's words, that "our fight is not against people on earth but against the rulers and authorities and the powers of this world's darkness" (Ephesians 6:12 NCV).

Your courage will be tested in your willingness to endure opposition, even persecution. The more you confront the status quo, the more people may criticize you, marginalize you, and vilify you. Jesus offered these words of encouragement: "People will insult you and hurt you. They will lie and say all kinds of evil things about you because you follow me. But when they do, you will be happy. Rejoice and be glad, because you have a great reward waiting for you in heaven" (Matthew 5:11–12 NCV).

> Courage has a number of facets to it: the willingness to oppose, the willingness to be opposed, the willingness to wait, and the willingness to not give up.

The New Rebellion is made of men and women who will not back down when it comes to righteousness, who will not conform mindlessly to generational currents. Courage is not blind, but is directed purposefully by God. It is not reckless, but walks in obedient submission to the Holy Spirit. Courage embraces risk for the reward of the Kingdom.

Courage

the insight

The willingness to wait and not give up is highlighted in the life of a courageous man named Joshua.

No, not *that* Joshua. Not the guy who brought down Jericho, but a guy who helped Ezra and Nehemiah lead fifty thousand Jews out of exile in Persia back into their Palestine homeland in 536 BC. The very effort to journey back to Israel required a good measure of courage. It meant uprooting the only life most of them had known, facing uncertain dangers and no real promises once they did get back. Many weighed the risks and decided to stay behind.

> You must be willing to undergo the pain of waiting, when it feels as if God has given up on you.

But not Joshua. His heritage and his passion had prepared him for this adventure, had prepared him to take the new role of high priest in the temple. There was one problem, however: There was no temple! The temple would have to be built, and it would be a long, arduous process. But their vision burned brightly, and they tackled the temple foundation with gusto. The foundation had just been completed when a new king came to power, and their work was forcibly halted.

No problem, they must have thought. *God has brought us this far, and He will work all this out.* But a year slipped by . . . then five . . . then ten. Fifteen years later, Joshua was starting to lose hope that he would ever see this temple he dreamed of. Enemies he could face, but this interminable waiting was stretching his courage to the breaking point.

So God gave a prophetic vision to Zechariah. In this vision, Joshua was standing before the throne of God. Satan was also there, hurling accusations at Joshua—perhaps things like, "You are such a joke! Your life is a failure. All your grand hopes are simply fabrications of your own imagination!" The Lord broke in and shut him up: "The LORD rebuke you, Satan!" (Zechariah 3:2 NKJV).

He went a step further and took off the dirty clothes Joshua was wearing and replaced them with a brand-new beautiful outfit. Then God reaffirmed Joshua's destiny: If you won't give up, God will establish you in the temple and fulfill the calling on your life. This is the courage God calls you to as well. You must be willing to undergo the pain of waiting, when it feels as if God has given up on you. Courage is often found in the simple determination to not give up.

Courage

the point

Courage has many faces. Is yours one of them? Have you learned to fight the right battles and in the right way? Many Christians get derailed here and wind up fighting people instead of ideas, fighting with anger instead of love. Courage is the willingness to submit yourself to God and resist the enemy (see James 4:7), to endure persecution, and to never let go of the purposes of God, even when they are a long time coming.

the talk

Courage is contagious. When a brave man takes a stand, the spines of others are often stiffened.

BILLY GRAHAM

Courage is the strength or choice to begin a change. Determination is the persistence to continue in that change.

ANONYMOUS

We must build dikes of courage to hold back the flood of fear.

MARTIN LUTHER KING JR.

Decision is a risk rooted in the courage of being free.

PAUL TILLICH

the word

Have I not commanded you? Be strong and of good courage; do not be afraid, nor be dismayed, for the LORD your God is with you wherever you go.

Joshua 1:9 NKJV

Watch, stand fast in the faith, be brave, be strong. Let all that you do be done with love.

1 Corinthians 16:13–14 NKJV

"Courage, it's me. Don't be afraid." Peter, suddenly bold, said, "Master, if it's really you, call me to come to you on the water." He said, "Come ahead."

Matthew 14:27–29 MSG

Christ is faithful as a Son over God's house. And we are God's house if we keep on being very sure about our great hope.

Hebrews 3:6 NCV

I know your persistence, your courage in my cause, that you never wear out.

Revelation 2:3 MSG

When they saw the boldness of Peter and John, and perceived that they were uneducated and untrained men, they marveled. And they realized that they had been with Jesus. . . . So when they had further threatened them, they let them go, finding no way of punishing them, because of the people, since they all glorified God for what had been done.

Acts 4:13, 21 NKJV

As for me, I trust in You O Lord; I say, "You are my God." My times are in Your hand . . . Oh, love the Lord, all you His saints! For the Lord preserves the faithful, and fully repays the proud person. Be of good courage, and He shall strengthen your heart, all you who hope in the Lord.

Psalm 31:14–15, 23–24 NKJV

Courage

the courage tools

Read it . . .

Breaking Intimidation
John Bevere
Establishing the grip of God and
breaking the grip of fear.

Can You Drink the Cup?
Henri Nouwen
Embracing the sweetness and bitterness
of life.

The Fear of the Lord
John Bevere
Intimately knowing and courageously
following God.

For Kirk and Covenant
Douglas Wilson
The stalwart courage of John Knox.

The Source of My Strength
Charles Stanley
His journey through grief and pain.

Voices of the Faithful
Beth Moore
Inspiring stories of courage from
Christians around the world.

**When People Are Big and
God Is Small**
Edward Welch
Overcoming the fear of people.

Surf it . . .

www.courage.org
Courage to overcome physical
handicaps.

www.mawhorter.org/radical/tiki
Collaborative discussion on
radical Christianity.

www.pregnancysupport.org
Courage to walk through
unmarried pregnancy.

Hear it . . .

Bethany Dillon, Bethany Dillon

His Strength Is Perfect,
Steven Curtis Chapman

Never Looking Back, Vineyard

Rachael Lampa, Rachael Lampa

Undone, Mercy Me

Where I Wanna Be, Vienna

Wire, Third Day

Do it . . .

Dare to Go Deeper conference,
www.family.org.

**Vision, resources, and events to
promote courageous manhood**,
www.bandofbrothers.org.

TOP TEN

The Top Ten Steps to Cultivate Courage

10   Identify your calling.

9   Identify your fears.

8   Consider how your fears will thwart your calling.

7   Consider the authority of Christ over your fears.

6   Trust God's ability rather than your limitations.

5   Decide whether you want a life of compliance or rebellion.

4   Always choose obedience in the face of fear.

3   Join forces with others of similar calling.

2   Remind yourself that God's side wins!

1   Embrace the adventure of a life of significance.

Courage is not simply one of the virtues, but the form of every virtue at the testing point.

C. S. Lewis

The Question

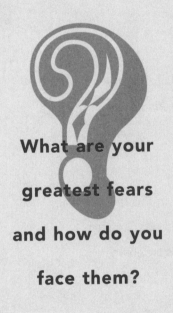

What are your greatest fears and how do you face them?

Failure? Ridicule? Falling? Do you really know your fears?

Courage is not the absence of fear; rather, it is the willingness to walk through your fears. The person who does not understand his or her fears is not yet fully capable of courage.

It's easier to deny fear than to engage it. It's easier to admit fear from a healthy distance than to grapple with it. Fortunately, God fully understands your fears and is exceedingly patient with the process of your coming to grips with them. He knows what you are able to bear at any given point in time. But when the time is right, He will require you to face them. Why? Because He wants you to rule them!

How was it that Jesus described His mission? "I have come that they may have life, and that they may have it more abundantly" (John 10:10 NKJV). Jesus is bigger than your fears, and He has made your heart His home. He wants to walk you right into the middle of your fears in order to show you that He is Lord of them. This is what the book of Proverbs calls, somewhat ironically, the "fear of the LORD" (1:7 NKJV). It is not a fear that terrifies or paralyzes; rather, it is the deepest quality of awe and adoration. It is, in essence, a dedication to the passion of God above every other passion.

> The person who does not understand his or her fears is not yet fully capable of courage.

When David wrote his psalm of greatest comfort, Psalm 23, he described a table of incredible supply. Yet that table was located right smack in the middle of enemies. Is this by accident? Not hardly! God intends to release your Kingdom destiny in such a way that you are no longer intimidated by the forces that once ruled you, by the things that continue to rule others in this world. Abundant life is your calling and your message.

Research has shown that one's thought life influences every aspect of one's being. Whether we are filled with confidence or fear depends on the kind of thoughts that habitually occupy our minds.
John Ortberg

Courage Under Fire

SAINT JOAN OF ARC
1412–1431

Refusal to take risks makes for a life of mediocrity at best.

Michael LeBoeuf

Joan was born into a complicated ancient world in eastern France. As a child, the shaky truce between England and France fell apart as King Henry V invaded France to claim the throne of that country for himself. When Joan was twelve, she began to have spiritual visions of saints and angels that forged a spiritual identity upon her from her youth.

At the mere age of sixteen, she felt God calling her to lead an army against the English and Burgundians (French sympathizers). Charles VII, rightful heir to the French throne, was doing poorly in warfare against Henry, but he was reluctant to take Joan seriously. Apparently, Joan was able to convince Charles of her legitimacy by recounting in great detail the contents of his prayers the night before, and she was subsequently given honorary command of his army.

Joan began an immediate overhaul of both morale and morality among the troops—throwing out prostitutes, requiring soldiers to attend church and confession, and setting new standards for behavior and military discipline. The effect was quite profound. As the army won its first skirmish, Joan distinguished herself in two ways that became her trademark: first, she carried a banner rather than a weapon; and second, she courageously placed herself in the same danger as the troops she led.

Success continued for Joan as she led the French in battle over the next two years. But the Burgundians rallied, and conflict persisted. At the city of Compiègne, Joan was cut off from her army and captured. Charles made frantic attempts at negotiating her return, but it was in vain. After four months in prison, she was given to the English in exchange for a tidy sum and brought before the Inquisition. She was eventually convicted of heresy and burned at the stake. She was only nineteen years old, but she was a world-changer.

wisdom from the past

Our love to God is measured
by our everyday fellowship with
others and the love it displays.

Andrew Murray

A Sacrificial Commitment

Love is intimidating. It is the most mystical and heavenly expression of the Kingdom you can know. And, of course, Jesus set the bar very high when it comes to love. And souls intuitively know how far short they fall.

Still, love is the one power that will change the world, and God is intent upon establishing His love as the consuming motivation and empowering liberation for every man, woman, and child who chooses to represent Him on planet Earth. When authentic love is encountered, everyone present knows that something of heaven has come to earth.

The redemption of salvation is a restoration to love—the ability to both receive an outrageous love from God and in turn give it away. To love well requires both sacrifice and service.

the buzz

Love. Jesus said it was the greatest commandment. In fact, He said that love was the fulfillment of the entire law of God. The Bible even says that God *is* love, setting love into a class all its own. Jesus told His disciples that unifying love would be the one force to show the world that the church was a manifestation of heavenly reality. So far, the thousands of rifts and divisions that have splintered the church of Jesus into hundreds of denominations haven't been very compelling to the world. We can do better.

But what is love, really? And how can we express it as Christ did? Heavenly love lies outside human capacity—it requires heavenly intervention and Kingdom fuel. At its core, love is an enduring commitment to live for another's good. This orientation toward others cuts across the inherent human tendency to self-centeredness. It is a constant choice—a constant dying, even—to lay down your own selfish desire in exchange for the opportunity to bring good to another.

Not only this, but living for another's good requires great discernment to know what that good is and how to contribute to it effectively. Many foolish and damaging things have been done in the name of

Jesus answered, " 'Love the Lord your God with all your heart, all your soul, and all your mind.' This is the first and most important command. And the second command is like the first: 'Love your neighbor as you love yourself.' "

Matthew 22:37–39 NCV

love—having premarital sex, enabling alcoholism, and spoiling children, just to name a few. These are cases where the intention may have been good, but the wisdom to deliver good was absent. Real love involves both intention and ability.

This ability to love well expresses itself in two dimensions: Love sacrifices courageously and serves redemptively, just as Jesus did. Love is willing and ready to put itself in harm's way for a greater good. It gladly accepts discomfort and personal cost if that will genuinely contribute to another's good. At the same time, love serves in such a way as to bring out the best in others. Love calls forth people's true identities and destinies.

> At its core, love is an enduring commitment to live for another's good. This orientation toward others cuts across the inherent human tendency to self-centeredness.

In your own pursuit of a life of love, ask yourself these questions: Who has God brought into my life for me to show the love of Christ? What sacrifices am I willing to bear in order to be a blessing in their lives? And how can I be a redemptive force, enabling God's Kingdom purposes to come forth for them?

As God deposits His love inside you, you will find yourself drawn by His Spirit to live for the good of others, even when that comes at personal cost to yourself. You will begin to discern how to love others well and then move to restore brokenness and release purpose in the ones you love.

the insight

Abigail was the wife of a wealthy man, and the Bible describes her in radiant terms: "intelligent and beautiful" (1 Samuel 25:3 NIV). But there was a problem—her husband, Nabal, was "surly and mean" (verse 3). This meant, of course, a very difficult life for Abigail, who, despite her great abilities, would likely be treated little better than a servant. The amazing thing is that this did not stop her from loving her husband and treating him with honor when the going got tough.

> Abigail was willing to protect her man, who arguably deserved the judgment David was bringing, and to bear that cost herself.

And it did get tough. Here's how it went down. David was pre-king and living as an outlaw with about six hundred warriors. They had been enforcing justice and protecting the inhabitants of the region, including Nabal, his men, and his property—and Nabal's men all knew it. David's provisions ran low just as Nabal was preparing an enormous feast, so David sent men to ask Nabal if he would share his feast with them. However, Nabal mocked David's men and spurned their request.

David, who felt dishonored and badly repaid for the service they had rendered, armed four hundred of his men to pay Nabal a little visit. Meanwhile, Abigail heard the whole story from her servants, who were themselves horrified at their master's behavior. Knowing that disaster was imminent, she took it on herself to gather an immense gift of food for David's men and delivered it to them—without Nabal's knowledge.

When she met David, she threw herself on the ground, saying, "My master, let the blame be on me!" (1 Samuel 25:24 NCV). This was the sacrificial side of her love: Abigail was willing to protect her man, who arguably deserved the judgment David was bringing, and to bear that cost herself, even to the loss of her life.

Abigail went on to affirm the call on David's life and to put her intervention in a redemptive light: "The LORD will keep all his promises of good things for you. He will make you leader over Israel. Then you won't feel guilty or troubled because you killed innocent people" (1 Samuel 25:30–31 NCV).

Throughout her traumatic ordeal, Abigail moved in love toward both her husband and David. In sacrificial risk as well as redemptive service, she proved herself a blessing to both. Nabal's life was spared, and David's conscience was spared, all because of one woman's wise love.

Love

the point

Abigail showed an enduring commitment to live for another's good, and so can you. No matter how you have been treated, you can love in return. Jesus calls you to love even your enemies! Love is not merely compliance; love is moving in such a way that blesses the people in your life. Love sacrifices, love discerns, and love redeems. In short, love is the prime directive for God's Kingdom.

the talk

In the evening of life we shall be judged on love, and not one of us is going to come off very well, and were it not for my absolute faith in the loving forgiveness of my Lord I could not call on him to come.

MADELEINE L'ENGLE

Our love to God is measured by our everyday fellowship with others and the love it displays.

ANDREW MURRAY

There is more hunger for love and appreciation in this world than for bread.

MOTHER TERESA

The best and most beautiful things in the world cannot be seen or even touched. They must be felt with the heart.

HELEN KELLER

Am I not destroying my enemies when I make friends of them?

ABRAHAM LINCOLN

the word

Love is patient and kind. Love is not jealous, it does not brag, and it is not proud. Love is not rude, is not selfish, and does not get upset with others. Love does not count up wrongs that have been done. Love is not happy with evil but is happy with the truth.

1 Corinthians 13:4–6 NCV

Trust steadily in God, hope unswervingly, love extravagantly. And the best of the three is love.

1 Corinthians 13:13 MSG

I tell you that her many sins are forgiven, so she showed great love. But the person who is forgiven only a little will love only a little.

Luke 7:47 NCV

A new commandment I give to you, that you love one another; as I have loved you, that you also love one another. By this all will know that you are My disciples, if you have love for one another.

John 13:34–35 NKJV

I pray that you and all God's holy people will have the power to understand the greatness of Christ's love—how wide and how long and how high and how deep that love is. Christ's love is greater than anyone can ever know, but I pray that you will be able to know that love.

Ephesians 3:18–19 NCV

I may speak in different languages of people or even angels. But if I do not have love, I am only a noisy bell or a crashing cymbal . . . I may have faith so great I can move mountains. But even with all these things, if I do not have love, then I am nothing . . . I may even give my body as an offering to be burned. But I gain nothing if I do not have love.

1 Corinthians 13:1–3 NCV

Love

the love tools

Read it . . .

A Love Worth Giving
Max Lucado
Portraits and stories from
1 Corinthians 13.

After God's Own Heart
Mike Bickle
Falling in love with a God who
loves you.

Lessons from a Sheep Dog
Phillip Keller
A true story of transforming love.

Loving God
Chuck Colson
Obedience and discipleship as the
path of love.

**Loving Your City into the
Kingdom**
Ted Haggard and Jack Hayford
City-reaching strategies for
twenty-first-century revival.

Messy Spirituality
Michael Yaconelli
God's annoying love for imperfect
people.

Servant Evangelism
Steve Sjogren
Winning the world by simple acts
of kindness.

Surf it . . .

www.allaboutgod.com/christian-love.
htm
Article on love as a lifestyle.

www.christiananswers.net/love/home
Resources for purity in sexual love.

www.christiancourier.com/archives/
agape
A study on the quality of God's love.

Hear it . . .

Adoration, Newsboys

All Right Here, Sara Groves

I Choose You, Point of Grace

See the Light, True Vibe

Testify to Love, Avalon

This Is Love, Vineyard Music

Who We Are Instead, Jars of Clay

Do it . . .

Put your love in action globally,
www.missiontreks.com.

Show love to needy children,
www.worldvision.org.

Love people practically,
www.servantevangelism.com.

TOP TEN

The Top Ten Ways to Love When It's Hard

10 Pray regularly for that person, even if he feels like an enemy.

9 Look for practical ways to serve him, even if he doesn't know.

8 Be available; time is the most precious gift you can offer.

7 Take opportunities to honor and speak well of that one.

6 Include him, when appropriate, in special activities.

5 Sometimes a hug or brief touch can communicate what words cannot.

4 Take the risk to share your heart with that person; be the real you.

3 If possible, worship or pray together or in a small group.

2 Journal your desire for God's good in his life.

1 Thank God for changing you through that person.

All the law is fulfilled in one word, even in this:
"You shall love your neighbor as yourself."

Galatians 5:14 NKJV

The Question

Who in your life do you find really hard to love, and how can you see him with God's perspective?

The truth is, there is almost always someone. Someone that just grates on you, whose personality rubs you the wrong way, something that you'd just rather not deal with in your life. And yet you have to. Maybe that someone is in your church. Maybe he or she is in your family. Maybe he works with you. Whatever the case, God chose to place that person in your life, and now you have to learn how to love him. That's not always an easy task.

Unifying love is the one thing that will convince the world that heaven has infiltrated earth. Not megachurches. Not political power. Not control of the media. Only one thing trumpets across the landscape of planet Earth that Christianity is the real deal: love. And this is why love is the very fabric of the New Rebellion.

You know something? You can burn

278

with a vision for love but not love. God is the One who takes your feeble attempts and breathes upon them with empowering grace to enable you to love someone who seems unlovely.

First, you must see yourself through the lens of grace and realize that you, too, were unlovely—but you are loved. By God and by a number of special people. Next, acknowledge your own inability to love in your own strength. Then ask God to download His perspective, His passion for this person into your heart. Ask Him to allow you the privilege of seeing this person's potential, the image of God in that one, through the eyes of the Holy Spirit.

> **L**ove is the very fabric of the New Rebellion.

It takes surrender, it takes courage, and it takes obedience. But the reward is heaven itself. The Kingdom leaps forward in every act of hidden, selfless love. What may be imperceptible in the earthly realm rocks the spiritual world with divine power and joy. Try it and see.

Beloved, if God so loved us, we also ought to love one another. No one has seen God at any time. If we love one another, God abides in us, and His love has been perfected in us.
1 John 4:11–12 NKJV

Courage Meets Humility

SAINT PATRICK
389–461

The early Irish Christianity planted in Ireland by Patrick is much more joyful and celebratory [than its Roman predecessor] in the way it approaches the natural world. It is really not a theology of sin but of the goodness of creation, and it really is intensely incarnational.

Thomas Cahill

At the age of sixteen, British-born Patrick was captured by pirates and sold into slavery in Ireland—a tragic beginning that God would later redeem for His good purpose. After six miserable years, Patrick was able to escape and return home, much to his relief. It was stunning, therefore, to receive a dream some years later in which God told him to return to the land of his sufferings. In the dream, he heard the Irish pleading with him, "Holy boy, we are asking you to come home and walk among us again." Struck by compassion, Patrick immediately obeyed.

The very slavery that interrupted Patrick's life was the catalyst that breathed a profound conversion into the dry, nominal faith of his upbringing and became a lifelong passion for the spiritual renewal of Ireland. Interrupted also in his education, Patrick retained an ongoing feeling of inferiority due to his lack of higher learning. But God used that for good as well, bringing forth a unique humility and approachability in his ministry that made him Ireland's most beloved spiritual figure for centuries.

Patrick's humility and strength won his way into the hearts of a nation that had no prior knowledge of or value for the gospel of Jesus. Overrun by paganism and witchcraft, Patrick single-handedly introduced them to a higher love. In all, he baptized more than 120,000 Irishmen and established at least 300 churches.

Although most known for bringing faith in Christ to a nation, Patrick was equally passionate for the cause of the poor, those marginalized by society, and for women. Due to his own firsthand experience, he became the first person in the history of the world to publicly challenge slavery; remarkably, by his death, slavery actually was abolished in Ireland, never to be revived. The legacy of Patrick was immense, but in the end, he simply gave them himself, and he showed them what love is.

wisdom from the past

I want deliberately to encourage this mighty longing after God. The lack of it has brought us to our present low estate. The stiff and wooden quality about our religious lives is a result of our lack of holy desire. Complacency is a deadly foe of all spiritual growth. Acute desire must be present or there will be no manifestation of Christ to His people. He waits to be wanted. Too bad that with many of us He waits so long, so very long, in vain.

C. S. Lewis

Belief in Motion

Passion has become something of a buzzword lately, and for good reason. For too long the church has been held captive in the domain of the mind. Right thinking—followed closely by right behavior—has been the goal of the Christian faith. Correct doctrine was the "holy grail" of the modern era, while emotions were merely tolerated in small measure, usually subjected to suspicion. The mind is safe, but emotions are dangerous!

But the same God who fabricated the mind also formed the emotions. And together they reflect the image of God in the souls of men and women everywhere. Passion has finally returned from exile to rejoin its more staid sibling, belief, in a potent blend that propels the New Rebellion into its time on the stage of planet Earth.

Passion is belief in motion.

Passion

1 the buzz

Belief is essential to every Christ-follower. Belief is the entry into relationship with God and isn't simply a mind-based agreement. Belief is a whole-life embrace of Christ. Yet belief without passion is suffocation. Belief that does not take flight in emotional expression becomes quickly dwarfed and shrunken, a pathetic monument to what might have been. The relationship with God does not cease, but neither does it go anywhere; it's like a marriage that never leaves the altar to begin living.

There is a part of your life with God that is intimate and hidden. The psalmist calls it the "secret place": "In the secret place of His tent He will hide me" (Psalm 27:5 NASB). "You hide them in the secret place of Your presence from the conspiracies of man; You keep them secretly in a shelter from the strife of tongues" (Psalm 31:20 NASB). This is where the flame is kindled. But if kept here, it will suffocate.

Whom have I in heaven but You? And there is none upon earth that I desire besides You. My flesh and my heart fail; but God is the strength of my heart and my portion forever.
Psalm 73:25–26 NKJV

When fanned into passionate flame, your life with God becomes a holy force to be reckoned with. It gives off heat; it gives off light. It has the power to consume, change, and transform its surroundings. The psalmist described this side as well: "I will tell of Your name to my brethren; in the midst of the assembly I will praise You" (Psalm 22:22

NASB). "Men shall speak of the power of Your awesome acts, and I will tell of Your greatness" (Psalm 145:6 NASB).

Passion is the freedom to let belief out of the closet of the mind where it can draw fresh oxygen into its lungs and start living life. Passion, by definition, moves beyond what is expected or considered normal. It draws attention to itself—perhaps for good, perhaps not—but it is never hidden. Passion without direction becomes a loose cannon and, through its power, can cause more harm than good. So, the greater the passion, the greater the wisdom needed to harness that powerful expression to the building of God's Kingdom.

> When fanned into passionate flame, your life with God becomes a holy force to be reckoned with.

So how do you navigate belief and passion? Ground yourself in the truth of God's Word. Receive trusted instruction so that your belief can grow strong and wise. Then let the Holy Spirit catapult your belief into passionate flight for Kingdom purpose. Your passion will affect the way you worship—it may look extreme, but it will be authentic. It will affect the way you pray and serve. It will affect your marriage and your family. Passion will release you to share your faith without fear.

Passion

the insight

Consider one of Scripture's most passionate men of all time—King David. His passion made him great, as both a warrior and a worshiper. It set him apart from the masses that protected the status quo. His passion, when cut loose from his belief, also caused destruction. But David learned from his mistakes—just as you do—and "served God's purpose in his own generation" (Acts 13:36 NIV). Look at one remarkable story of his passion.

> David was a humble man and allowed his passion to be refined, not extinguished.

After David was finally made king, he established his palace and began to build the nation. Before long, he desired to bring the ark of the covenant—the symbol of God's presence—up from Judah into Jerusalem where it could be placed in honor. It's important to recognize that David's passion was directed righteously; his hunger for God and God's rule motivated this plan.

However, in his passion he failed to follow the prescribed laws for moving the ark in an honorable way. He used a cart instead of having the Levites carry it on their shoulders. In this case, David's passion got disconnected from his belief in the word of God. As a result, the cart lurched. A man named Uzzah reached to steady the ark and was struck dead by God for dishonoring it. But David was a humble man and allowed his passion to be refined, not extinguished.

He brought in the Levites, followed God's commands, and brought the ark into Jerusalem with tremendous celebration. Then his passion caught fire: David threw off his royal robe and in his simple tunic began to leap and dance and yell praises. But this was not how kings were "supposed to behave," and his wife, Michal, was angry because her pride suffocated her passion.

She confronted him with sarcasm: "With what honor the king of Israel acted today! You took off your clothes in front of the servant girls of your officers like one who takes off his clothes without shame!" (2 Samuel 6:20 NCV). But David defended his passion: "I will celebrate in the presence of the LORD. Maybe I will lose even more honor, and maybe I will be brought down in my own opinion, but the girls you talk about will honor me!" (2 Samuel 6:21–22 NCV). And God judged Michal for her lack of passion by not allowing her to have any children.

Passion

the point

God wants to activate your passion as an empowering force for your Kingdom calling. Don't be ashamed of it. Don't hold back the exuberance of your emotions toward God. But do allow it to be grounded and directed by truth and wisdom. Your passion may bring disapproval from people, but if it is the authentic expression of your belief, it will bring approval from God. And it's His opinion that counts.

the talk

All who call on God in true faith, earnestly from the heart, will certainly be heard, and will receive what they have asked and desired.

MARTIN LUTHER

There is no emptiness of soul ever for those whose life is devoted to God.

WILLIAM LAWSON

We are at this moment as close to God as we really choose to be. True, there are times when we would like to know a deeper intimacy, but when it comes to the point, we are not prepared to pay the price involved.

J. OSWALD SAUNDERS

Few delights can equal the mere presence of One whom we fully trust.

GEORGE MACDONALD

the word

You're blessed when you've worked up a good appetite for God. He's food and drink in the best meal you'll ever eat.

Matthew 5:6 MSG

Those who want to save their lives will give up true life, and those who give up their lives for me will have true life.

Matthew 16:25 NCV

As the deer pants for the water brooks, so pants my soul for You, O God. My soul thirsts for God, for the living God. When shall I come and appear before God?

Psalm 42:1–2 NKJV

He said to those who were selling pigeons, "Take these things out of here! Don't make my Father's house a place for buying and selling!" When this happened, the followers remembered what was written in the Scriptures: "My strong love for your Temple completely controls me."

John 2:16–17 NCV

If you love me, you will obey my commands.

John 14:15 NCV

Passion

the passion tools

Read it . . .

Desiring God
John Piper
The pleasures of Christian hedonism:
God!

First Love
Bill Bright
Renewing your passion for God.

The Glorious Pursuit
Gary Thomas
Embracing the virtues of Christ.

The God Chasers
Tommy Tenney
A life of hunger that exceeds your reach.

The Love Languages of God
Gary Chapman
How to feel and reflect divine love.

One Holy Passion
R. C. Sproul
The consuming thirst to know God.

Passion for Jesus
Mike Bickle
A glimpse into God's overriding
passion for you.

Pleasures Evermore
Sam Storms
A guidebook to happy holiness.

Surf it . . .

www.desiringgod.org
God-intoxicated resources from John
Piper.

www.intouch.org/teen
The Teen Connection for passionate
youth.

Hear it . . .

Beautiful World, Take 6
Bold, Angie and Debbie Winans
Cry Holy, Sonic Flood
Desire, Vineyard Music
Disappear, PFR
Keith Green: The Ultimate Collection,
Keith Green
Life's a Ride, Carol Frazier
Millennial Swing, Swing Music

Do it . . .

Passion conference and events,
www.worshiptogether.com/events.

*Passionate events and missions for
youth*, www.teenmania.com.

TOP TEN

The Top Ten Expressions of a Passionate Faith

10 Worship freely: Let your body mirror your soul.

9 Pray continually: Speak with feeling and intensity.

8 Share openly: Do not filter your spirituality around unbelievers.

7 Live intentionally: Fill every day with Kingdom content.

6 Serve radically: Lead your family into spiritual connection.

5 Love deeply: Look for and respond to people's urgent needs.

4 Listen carefully: Take the time to hear people's true hearts.

3 Protect vigilantly: Know the enemy's schemes and cut him off.

2 Speak honestly: Don't mask your soul in religious veneer.

1 Rest thankfully: Invest wisely in Sabbath renewal.

The Question

- →

Are you feeling a consistent hunger for more of God or do you find yourself satisfied with lesser things?

How do you feel when you take a bite of a luscious brownie or a juicy hamburger? You can't wait to take another, and then to finish it off entirely. Right? Does being with God, just experiencing His presence, make you feel that way? Do you find yourself excited in worship, anticipating His nearness, enthusiastic when you talk about His work in your life? These are the telltale signs of passion.

Appetite is always an indicator of health. When a person loses his desire for food, it is a glaring wake-up call that the body is sick and needs healing. The same is true in your spiritual health: It's like taking your spiritual temperature, like checking your vital signs. Do you yearn for time in your Christian community? Do you desire to make a difference in your world today? Are you passionate to share the things God has been teaching you with others?

Of course, no one is wide-open passionate all the time. It's normal for feelings to ebb and flow. But it's also important to know the average level of spiritual hunger that characterizes your life so that you can live true to your spiritual destiny. When feelings are low, your core beliefs allow you to hold your course and not be shipwrecked by the siren call of other destructive appetites.

It should be of little surprise that this world and its spiritual forces try to lure you away from your true passion with glittery substitutes. There are many things that sate the soul and bring temporary pleasure; but like junk food, the satisfaction fades quickly and leaves a dull ache in its wake. In contrast, the pleasures of God bring lasting satisfaction that does not disappoint or leave a bad aftertaste.

Do you find yourself excited in worship, anticipating His nearness, enthusiastic when you talk about His work in your life?

What are you afraid of? Let God act. Abandon yourself to Him. You will suffer, but you will suffer with love, peace, and consolation. You will fight, but you can carry off the victory, and God Himself . . . will crown you with His own hand. You will weep, but your tears will be sweet, and God Himself will come with satisfaction to dry them.
François Fénelon

Prophet of Passion

KEITH GREEN
1954–1982

Keith was blunt, he was funny, he was tactless, and sometimes even crude. He steadfastly refused to accept the spiritual status quo. He was cut off by some and almost canonized by others—but he was impossible to ignore.

Winkie Pratney

"**I** repent of ever having recorded one single song, and ever having performed one concert, if my music, and more importantly, my life has not provoked you . . . to sell out more completely to Jesus!" This was the passion of Keith Green. Singer, storyteller, radical ambassador for Jesus. Few people have burned as fiercely—or as briefly—as this young seeker of the New Rebellion.

His musical genius emerged early, and like many other young hopefuls in the 1970s, Keith worked the club scene in Hollywood looking for the big break. But unlike many, he was desperate to discover real truth and earnestly searched all the religious venues of the day—from his own Jewish roots to Eastern mysticism, from psychedelic drug trips to Christian Science, and even to the Bible.

At the age of twenty-one, Keith's journey led him into the arms of Christ, and his passion intensified. His wife, Melody, wrote, "On the outside he looked like everyone else our age—but underneath it all he seemed out-of-step with the times. His ideas—even his whole character—seemed to be in opposition to the values that were so popular."

Keith's passion is perhaps captured best by one particular image. He was on the final night of a three-day ministry tour in Tulsa. God's Spirit had interrupted the music, and thousands were mobbing the stage in repentance. Keith stopped talking, and God was directing the show. Keith actually crawled underneath the nine-foot grand piano to cry and pray as God cleansed hearts and renewed their passion for Him. But the fire was not to last.

On July 28, 1982, Keith and two of his children were killed when their small plane crashed in the woods near their Texas home. The tragedy stunned an entire generation of people, young and old alike, who had been riveted by the passion of Keith's hunger for God. He had indeed awakened a generation.

wisdom from the past

I've discovered that highly effective people are not so much brilliant as balanced.

Alan Loy McGinnis

Strength for Body and Soul

Frequently those who are most zealous for the Kingdom life of the Spirit give the least attention to the health of their bodies. God assures His people that this is a mistake to be avoided. While the ancient Greeks emphasized the divisions of their humanity (body, soul, and spirit), the ancient Jews emphasized their unity of being and God's interest in all of it.

The Bible focuses most of its message toward spiritual issues, but there is also a periodic return to the importance of body and soul. In this way, God calls His new rebels to a holistic approach to redemption: His vision is for training in spirit and training in body, for healing of spirit and healing of body. And the earthly ministry of Jesus confirmed this balance. Today's Christ-followers will imitate this balance and be known for a passion and vitality that pervade every dimension of their being.

Health

1 the buzz

Whole-person health is more than mere pragmatism. Those who ignore or mistreat their bodies may not live long enough or be mobile enough to fulfill their spiritual destiny. That's a big deal. But a holistic approach to health goes beyond pragmatism to principle. Even if you could beat all the odds and never be limited by your body, the New Rebellion recognizes the fact that God cares deeply about the entirety of the person He has made you to be. Even your physical body.

God didn't skimp on your body—He didn't give it less attention or value than other aspects of your being. Your mind and emotions are incredibly complex and actually reflect the divine image in ways humans can't fully comprehend. God cares deeply about the entire package that makes up you. Because of this, health matters. Personal hygiene matters. Dress matters. Even manners matter.

The fact is that God has entrusted you with an extremely valuable set of resources—intellectual, social, physical, sexual, emotional, and spiritual. Every facet must be treated with respect and given wise attention and maintenance. This means that no matter how much you pray and read your Bible, you can't stuff your face with a

Even children become tired and need to rest, and young people trip and fall. But the people who trust the LORD will become strong again. They will rise up as an eagle in the sky; they will run and not need rest; they will walk and not become tired.
Isaiah 40:30–31 NCV

constant stream of junk food and remain in alignment with your Kingdom calling. You can't finish your education and then allow your mind to go dormant for the next sixty years. Both body and mind require lifelong care in order to enable lifelong obedience.

Your emotional life is also an essential part of the package. A staggering percentage of men and women in ministry get derailed from their calling due to relational stress and emotional burnout. These things can be avoided, especially with the breadth of counseling and soul-tools now available. Almost everyone requires healing from past emotional wounds before he or she can be released into effective ministry; that includes you. The fulfilling of your calling in life will hinge largely upon your ability to successfully engage in healthy relationships, so whatever investment you make in this department will give valuable returns.

God cares deeply about the entire package that makes up you. Because of this, health matters. Personal hygiene matters. Dress matters. Even manners matter.

Another gift of God to His children is sexuality, and while this topic doesn't tend to get much attention from the pulpit, it's part of who you are and is valuable to God. More than just keeping yourself from sexual sin, God invites you into sexual health: If you're not married, He invites you into a life of purity. If you are married, He invites you into sexual fulfillment as well as a continuing purity. Body, mind, and soul—it all belongs to God.

Health

the insight

When Nebuchadnezzar, king of Babylon, took the nation of Judah into captivity, a contingent of Israelite nobility were brought into the Babylonian court to be trained in their language and literature for three years and then released into the king's service. Among those selected were four famous young men: Daniel, Shadrach, Meshach, and Abednego.

They are most well-known for their refusal to bow down to Nebuchadnezzar's idol and their subsequent miraculous deliverance when thrown into a raging furnace. But their courage began years before that, back when they were first enrolled in their training.

> Vegetables and water were considered peasants' fare, not the food of nobles. But the truth is that the same rules of health today applied in 605 BC as well. ntr

First of all, the whole basis of their selection was predicated upon the physical and mental health these men had pursued prior to their captivity. The result was that they were "handsome and well educated, capable of learning and understanding, and able to serve" (Daniel 1:4 NCV). Those healthy attributes weren't present by mere genetics but rather by commitment and discipline.

In addition to health of body and soul, they were vigilant toward health of spirit. Because the Babylonians' food and wine were ceremonially dedicated to their idols before serving it, Daniel and his friends knew they would be compromising the honor of God by eating and drinking it. There had to be another solution.

The steward in charge of their training was sympathetic to their convictions but laid it out plainly: The men had to remain strong and healthy, or it would be his head. God gave Daniel a creative idea, and he challenged the steward to give them a ten-day trial period. During that time, they would eat only vegetables and drink only water; then the steward could see the results for himself.

Vegetables and water were considered peasants' fare, not the food of nobles. But the truth is that the same rules of health today applied in 605 BC as well. The fresh vegetarian diet of those four men placed them in obvious superior condition to all the rest. Their point proved, the men continued to flourish on that diet for the next three years.

The unique destiny laid upon Daniel and his friends would not have been possible had they not taken as much consideration for their physical and mental health as they did for their spiritual health. As it turned out, their whole-person commitment to the service of God placed them in the position to affect their world in dramatic ways.

Health

the point

Your holistic commitment to bring your body, soul, and spirit into alignment with God's Kingdom purposes will qualify you for the destiny He has prepared for you. Guard your physical well-being through responsible eating and exercise. Activate your mind through a lifelong commitment to learning. Train your emotions to reflect the heartbeat of God in all you do. When every component of your being comes into agreement with a Godward life, your potential will be unleashed for God.

the talk

While we may not be called to martyr our lives, we must martyr our way of life. We must put our selfish ways to death and march to a different beat. Then the world will see Jesus.

MICHAEL TAIT

A good conscience is to the soul what health is to the body; it preserves constant ease and serenity within us; and more than countervails all the calamities and afflictions which can befall us from without.

JOSEPH ADDISON

We all live in a fallen world, are damaged, and need to be healed as we grow in our relationships with others and God.

DAN ALLENDER

True silence is the rest of the mind; it is to the spirit what sleep is to the body, nourishment and refreshment.

WILLIAM PENN

the word

Do you not know that your body is the temple of the Holy Spirit who is in you, whom you have from God, and you are not your own? For you were bought at a price; therefore glorify God in your body and in your spirit, which are God's.

1 Corinthians 6:19–20 NKJV

Unless the LORD builds the house, they labor in vain who build it; unless the LORD guards the city, the watchman stays awake in vain. It is vain for you to rise up early, to sit up late, to eat the bread of sorrows; for so He gives His beloved sleep.

Psalm 127:1–2 NKJV

Dear friend, I pray that you may enjoy good health and that all may go well with you, even as your soul is getting along well.

3 John 2 NIV

Don't depend on your own wisdom. Respect the LORD and refuse to do wrong. Then your body will be healthy, and your bones will be strong.

Proverbs 3:7–8 NCV

I discipline my body and bring it into subjection, lest, when I have preached to others, I myself should become disqualified.

1 Corinthians 9:27 NKJV

Well, it may be true that the body is only a temporary thing, but that's no excuse for stuffing your body with food, or indulging it with sex. Since the Master honors you with a body, honor him with your body! God honored the Master's body by raising it from the grave. He'll treat yours with the same resurrection power. Until that time, remember that your bodies are created with the same dignity as the Master's body.

1 Corinthians 6:13–15 MSG

Health

the health tools

Read it . . .

Basic Steps to Godly Fitness
Laurette Willis
Strengthening your body and soul in
Christ.

Greater Health God's Way
Stormie Omartian
Seven steps to inner and outer beauty.

Healing for Damaged Emotions
David Seamands
God's help for problems that hinder
spiritual growth.

The Healing Power of Prayer
Chester L. Tolson
The surprising connection between
prayer and your health.

Health 4 Life
Jody Wilkinson, M.D., M.S.
Fifty-five simple ideas for living
healthy: physical, spiritual, mental,
and emotional.

Invitation to Solitude and Silence
Ruth Haley Barton
Experiencing God's transforming
presence.

The Maker's Diet
Jordan Rubin
The forty-day health experiment
that will change your life.

Surf it . . .

groups.msn.com/ChristianFitness
Extensive resources on exercise and
nutrition.

www.ccrhouston.org
Sexual health—freedom from
homosexuality.

www.healthrecipes.com
Practical suggestions for daily nutrition.

Hear it . . .

The Boy vs. The Cynic, John Reuben

Curves, Freedom Fitness

Disciple, Disciple

Exodus, Plus One

Genesis, Joy Williams

Krystal Meyers, Krystal Meyers

Moving on Faith, Jadon Lavik

So Natural, Salvador

Do it . . .

**Resources, newsletter, recipes, and
more**, www.fit4jesus.com.

Spiritual and emotional healing,
www.theophostic.com.

TOP TEN

The Top Ten Ways to Enhance Your Health

10 Tame workaholism and stress through spiritual disciplines.

9 Protect your sleep as the gift of God.

8 Eat when you're hungry; stop when you're full.

7 Choose fresh, natural foods over processed ones.

6 Integrate moderate exercise to sharpen mind and body.

5 Seek balance between work and play, community and solitude.

4 Use godly resources for emotional and sexual health.

3 Keep your conscience clear of sin and unforgiveness.

2 Stimulate your mind through diverse reading and study.

1 Learn to listen to the condition of your body, soul, and spirit.

The Question

- →

What things do you choose to do or not to do because you understand that your body is important to God?

God has given you in your physical body an immeasurable gift that reflects the beauty of His matchless design and His customized calling, as well as His own image. It is a priceless work of art that demands care and love and protection. When you allow God's view of you to shape your own self-view, then you begin to relate to yourself in healthy, God-honoring ways. It's not about elevating yourself and worshiping your body; it's about stewarding the gift God entrusted you with.

This stewardship, when taken seriously, will make serious demands upon your behavior. You cannot neglect your body. You cannot abuse your body. You must *do* certain things and not do certain things. Do you know what those things are? He will speak them to you if you are willing to listen. The abuse of the body may be as severe as illegal drug use or drunkenness, but there are many other forms, including legal drug abuse, obesity, sleep deprivation, and smoking. God never comes in harsh judgment for these mistakes; instead, He invites you into the freedom of His Kingdom where the entire body, soul, and spirit are healed and renewed and empowered for purpose.

The path to freedom is the path of obedience. Listen to the appeal of the Spirit, and then take intentional steps to bring your body into alignment with God's vision for you. Decide which practices will build your emotional and physical health. Find a partner who will help you establish new habit patterns, someone who can appreciate the spiritual dimension of physical health. In prayer and practice, break old habit patterns that have compromised your freedom. Then embrace the organic accountability that comes through true Christian community, and pursue a lifestyle of whole-person health.

Find a partner who will help you establish new habit patterns, someone who can appreciate the spiritual dimension of physical health.

Concentrate on the qualities in other people that you can affirm, and dwell on those things instead of on their faults. This alone should do wonders in relieving stress in your relationships. Doctors know that prolonged anxiety harms you, but healing words can soothe stress, and a peaceful mind leads to improved physical health too.

Patricia Wagner

A Healed Healer

JORDAN RUBIN
Entrepreneur

Dr. Jordan Rubin is on a mission from God to change the health of this nation . . . I have been praying for more than a year that God would lead me to a health plan that was based on the Bible and tested by science.

Dr. Charles Stanley

A native of Palm Beach Gardens, Florida, Jordan Rubin was nineteen when first diagnosed with Crohn's disease and ulcerative colitis, an "incurable" inflammatory disease of the bowel. His weight plummeted from 180 pounds to 104 pounds for his six-one height, and he was bedridden for almost two years. As his immune system began to fail, he suffered from more than twenty different symptoms, including excruciating abdominal pain, chronic diarrhea, arthritis, chronic fatigue, insomnia, and depression.

Rubin sought the help of approximately seventy health professionals from seven countries and tried more than two hundred different alternative supplements. His illness did not respond to standard medicine or alternative medical approaches, and he was forced to drop out of college. Rubin finally arrived at death's door in 1996 as the most severe symptoms of Crohn's took their toll.

Finally, after trying everything else with no improvement, his chiropractor father sent him some information on soil bacteria. Rubin was intrigued and began taking a product that contained homeostatic soil organisms—basically good bacteria that optimize digestion and the immune system. For a few weeks he felt slightly worse, but after thirty days Jordan felt a sudden surge of energy, and his digestive problems began to disappear. Within three months he gained his weight back. Within four months his body began to heal itself.

Today, years after being diagnosed with an "incurable disease," Jordan Rubin has no trace of the disease that almost cost him his life. Jordan weighs 190 pounds and is very healthy and active. He exhibits no symptoms of his former disease. Now a doctor of naturopathic medicine, Rubin is the founder of the fastest-growing nutritional company in America. His passion is to teach others how to take control of their own health so they can live for the glory of God.

> [Moses] said, "You must obey the LORD your God and do what he says is right. If you obey all his commands and keep his rules, I will not bring on you any of the sicknesses I brought on the Egyptians. I am the LORD who heals you."
>
> Exodus 15:26 NCV

wisdom from the now

Spirit filled souls are ablaze for God. They love with a love that glows. They serve with a faith that kindles. They serve with a devotion that consumes. They hate sin with fierceness that burns. They rejoice with a joy that radiates. Love is perfected in the fire of God.

Samuel Chadwick

Obedience over Time

Commitment incorporates many vital character qualities that could collectively be termed "integrity," and then commitment applies those qualities over the long haul of life. Commitment is characterized largely by obedience and perseverance, and provides a zoomed-out, big-picture assessment of your spiritual life. In short, commitment is the grace to go the distance—to finish the race and to finish strong.

If passion is where the mind and emotions meet, commitment is the domain of the will. This is the place where God's own longevity is planted in the human heart and demonstrates the divine commitment to His will and His people. The value of commitment can be most accurately seen (as is true of most values) in the absence of it. Lack of commitment can absolutely destroy the Kingdom life God calls you to.

Commitment

the buzz

God's call to commitment speaks to both the breadth and the length of the Christian journey. On the breadth side, commitment is evidenced by a willingness to obey God in all aspects of life, not just a few. Every Christ-follower finds it easier to surrender to God and His Word in some areas of life than in others. And while everyone is in the process of being changed more and more into the image of Jesus, some people find a measure of contentment in compartmentalizing certain facets of life inside the realm of obedience and other facets outside the realm of obedience. This speaks to the lack of commitment in that individual.

[God] sent a man before them—Joseph— who was sold as a slave. They hurt his feet with fetters, he was laid in irons. Until the time that his word came to pass, the word of the LORD tested him.
Psalm 105:17–19 NKJV

The New Rebellion is an all-or-nothing proposition. It is a whole-life dedication to serve God above self and to yield oneself entirely to the direction of the King. It neither requires nor expects perfection, fortunately, but it makes a claim upon every fiber of one's being. It is not for the faint of heart, but for those committed to God's agenda on planet Earth. It is for those who are willing to be set apart from the crowd and consecrated to the service of God.

Commitment speaks to the breadth of the Christian journey but also to the length of it. In this way, it combines both a quality of life and a quantity of life—a life that doesn't peter out but is sustained through time and circumstance. It does not flourish for a while but then dry up and fade away. Everyone knows people who have done that very thing: They talked the talk and even seemed to walk the walk, but it didn't last. Time tests the fruit of every life and gives assurance that the roots are healthy and firmly in place.

Hardship and difficulty also test the quality of every man's or woman's commitment. Almost every biblical player in the Kingdom of God had a "desert experience"—usually one that lasted for years. Abraham's testing time lasted twenty-five years. Joseph's lasted thirteen. Moses had forty years. And if that weren't enough, he got another forty years on top of that. If those mighty men of faith had to learn commitment through the testing of time and difficulty, you can also reasonably expect to have your commitment tested and proved.

The New Rebellion is an all-or-nothing proposition. It is a whole-life dedication to serve God above self and to yield oneself entirely to the direction of the King.

Consider both the breadth and length of your own walk with Christ. Is it inclusive? Does it empower your whole life experience? And how has it held up under time and obstacles? True identity and destiny can weather all the storms that invariably come and will be affirmed, not diminished.

Commitment

the insight

If ever a man had the calling to be a world-changer, it was Joseph. Although the youngest of twelve brothers, Joseph held his father's affection in a unique way. You will remember the multicolored coat he received from his father, Jacob, as a tangible expression of that favor. More than that, he had the favor of God, and through several prophetic dreams God spoke an impossibly large destiny over him.

> Tempted to political power and sexual sin, Joseph chose integrity. Tempted to discouragement and disillusionment with God, he persevered.

That dream was immediately and severely tested for thirteen long years. His brothers wanted to kill him, but instead they sold him to Egyptian slave traders. Purchased by a wealthy merchant, Joseph rose to favor and authority within his household. But then he was falsely accused and sent to prison. In prison, favor again followed Joseph, and he rose to authority within that evil place. Accurately interpreting the royal baker's dream opened up the possibility that Joseph might be rescued; instead, he was forgotten.

The commitment Joseph displayed throughout that arduous experience demonstrates both the breadth and length of Joseph's character. Tempted to political power and sexual sin, Joseph chose integrity. Tempted to discouragement and disillusionment with God, he persevered. The height of rulership God had in store for Joseph required that his spiritual commitment be tested long and hard. King David later wrote about this testing, "Until the time that his word [over Joseph] came to pass, the word of the LORD tested him" (Psalm 105:19 NKJV).

Another biblical window into the testing of commitment comes from Jesus' parable of the farmer scattering seed (see Matthew 13). He described four different kinds of soil as representative of the hearts of people. Some seed falls on the path—those people are hardened and don't respond to Jesus' invitation at all. Some seed falls on tilled, fertile soil—those people receive the message and are transformed by it.

But two types of soil represent people who fail in their commitment. Both receive the gospel with joy but don't last. One type has rocky soil, and no roots are established; upon meeting difficulty or persecution in their first encounter, they quit. The other soil is overrun with weeds that choke out the life of God with "cares and worries." Your commitment to the Kingdom will face these very challenges: *difficulty* and *distraction*. It takes courage and endurance to remain focused on what really matters and establish a commitment that can last a lifetime.

Commitment

the point

When the Bible invites believers into the life of the Spirit, it promises the "fruit" of the Spirit in their lives (see Galatians 5:22–23). Several of those fruit—patience, faithfulness, and self-control—are wrapped up in the word *commitment*. As you cultivate the Spirit's presence and freedom in your life, you can expect God to establish a backbone of commitment inside you: a commitment that brings obedience to every facet of your life and one that perseveres across every obstacle.

the talk

Confidence thrives on honesty, on honor, on the sacredness of obligations, on faithful protection and on unselfish performance. Without them it cannot live.

FRANKLIN D. ROOSEVELT

Obedience to the call of Christ nearly always costs everything to two people—the one who is called, and the one who loves that one.

OSWALD CHAMBERS

I have found that there are three stages in every great work of God: first, it is impossible, then it is difficult, then it is done.

HUDSON TAYLOR

I do not pray for success, I ask for faithfulness.

MOTHER TERESA

the word

Be careful in your life and in your teaching. If you continue to live and teach rightly, you will save both yourself and those who listen to you.

1 Timothy 4:16 NCV

When people are tempted and still continue strong, they should be happy. After they have proved their faith, God will reward them with life forever. God promised this to all those who love him.

James 1:12 NCV

Let us not grow weary while doing good, for in due season we shall reap if we do not lose heart.

Galatians 6:9 NKJV

My beloved brethren, be steadfast, immovable, always abounding in the work of the Lord, knowing that your labor is not in vain in the Lord.

1 Corinthians 15:58 NKJV

Keep your eyes open, hold tight to your convictions, give it all you've got, be resolute, and love without stopping.

1 Corinthians 16:13–14 MSG

Do everything without complaining or arguing. Then you will be innocent and without any wrong. You will be God's children without fault . . . You offer the teaching that gives life. So when Christ comes again, I can be happy because my work was not wasted. I ran the race and won. Your faith makes you offer your lives as a sacrifice in serving God. If I have to offer my own blood with your sacrifice, I will be happy and full of joy with all of you.

Philippians 2:14–17 NCV

Commitment

the commitment tools

Read it . . .

The Believer's Call to Commitment
Andrew Murray
A study from Ephesians on the Christian walk.

The Blessing of Commitment
Bobby Hilton
The divine results that follow whole-hearted obedience.

Commitment
Robert Boyd Munger
Bible study on this essential character quality.

The Divine Conspiracy
Dallas Willard
Rediscovering your hidden life in God.

Every Young Man, God's Man
Stephen Arterburn
Pursuing confidence, courage, and commitment.

Returning to Your First Love
Tony Evans
Reclaiming the spark of your passion for God.

A Ten Week Journey to Standing Firm
Donna Partow
God's power in the midst of overwhelming circumstances.

Surf it . . .

www.christiancentury.org
Online magazine on "Faithful living, Critical thinking."

www.iclnet.org
Electronic library of Christian resources.

www.radicalchristianity.org.uk
Committed to the original lifestyle of Jesus in the UK.

Hear it . . .

Be Thou My Vision, The Cambridge Singers

Brave, Nichole Nordeman

Desire, Vineyard Music

Engage, Pax 217

Even More, Anthony Evans

Fight the Tide, Sanctus Real

Wait for Me, Rebecca St. James

Where I Wanna Be, Vienna

Do it . . .

Commit to indigenous missions, www.christianaid.org.

Promise Keepers events for committed manhood, www.promisekeepers.org.

The Top Ten Practices to Sustain Your Commitment

10 Worship: Renew your vision of the one you love.

9 Remembrance: Remind yourself of God's past faithfulness.

8 Planning: Set goals and strategies toward your spiritual calling.

7 Prayer: Cultivate intimacy with the one you're committed to.

6 Fellowship: Jointly own each other's failures and successes.

5 Study: Use books and the Bible to equip and inspire.

4 Solitude: Reflect on your motivations for a life of faith.

3 Faith: Actively trust in the character and promises of God.

2 Meditation: Interpret the purposes of God in difficulty.

1 Passion: Put faith in motion to see the results of your commitment.

The Question

What sacrifices are you making for the more important issues and people in your life?

Commitment involves a never-ending series of choices. It means frequently saying no to the wrong things (even when they are good things) in order to say yes to the right things. So commitment relies heavily upon discernment in order to make those choices correctly, the discernment to know which people and activities are most important, most central to your spiritual calling.

Once the important things are clearly understood, then it requires certain sacrifices must be made to keep them in the priority position. Sacrifices of time, energy, money, thought, prayer, and so forth. These investments of your resources empower your commitment to live true to God's Kingdom. Without investing those resources sacrificially, all you're left with are good intentions.

God, family, church, vocation, friendships, prayer, exercise, entertainment—all of these have some value in your life. And almost everyone has, at one time or another, made a neat little list to try to prioritize the elements of his life. But let's be honest: Lists aren't very helpful when it comes to living. All the components that make up your life are intertwined in complicated array. It takes God's Spirit to speak and lead and make Kingdom priorities come to life in practical choices every day.

Investments of your resources empower your commitment to live true to God's Kingdom.

But His Spirit *does* live in you and *does* lead you and *will* empower your choices with Kingdom impact when you give Him that place of leadership. It does require selflessness and sacrifice, but the rewards more than make up for it! God's people will not be known for sad, drawn faces but for a contagious exuberance that captivates their souls. They will also reap the priceless gift of a life well lived. Lived intentionally. Lived sacrificially and gloriously. It was the joy that the Father set before Jesus that empowered His commitment to the Kingdom, and so it is yours.

We have around us many people whose lives tell us what faith means. So let us run the race that is before us and never give up. We should remove from our lives anything that would get in the way . . . Think about Jesus' example. He held on while wicked people were doing evil things to him. So do not get tired and stop trying.

Hebrews 12:1–3 NCV

One Committed Rebel

CORRIE TEN BOOM
1892–1983

Worry does not empty tomorrow of its sorrow. It empties today of its strength.

Corrie ten Boom

There was a simple ordinariness that belied the radical edge deep inside the ten Boom family. They served anyone who was in need, viewing their home as an open house and serving the needy among their community in Haarlem, Holland. When World War II erupted, their home became a refuge, a hiding place, for all those pursued by injustice—students who refused cooperation with the Nazis, members of the Dutch underground resistance, and, of course, Jews. The ten Booms lived out their faith with a fierce commitment to nonviolent resistance.

The gestapo raided the ten Boom home on February 28, 1944, waiting throughout the day to seize everyone coming into the house. Thirty people were arrested, including Corrie, her father, two sisters, a brother, and a nephew. And since underground materials were found in the house, the six members of the ten Boom family were all sent to prison. Corrie survived.

While Corrie and her sister Betsie inhabited the infamous Ravensbrück concentration camp near Berlin, life was brutal and oppressive. Yet in the midst of the hate and brutality, these two determined souls spent their time serving and loving their fellow prisoners, leading many to faith in Jesus. Their refrain became, "There is no pit so deep that God's love is not deeper still . . . God will give us the love to be able to forgive our enemies."

When Corrie was liberated from the death camp, she knew God had spared her life for a purpose and began a worldwide ministry at the age of fifty-three. It became her passion to communicate the love of God—a love that overcomes the fiercest hate and most unjust sufferings. The next thirty-three years allowed Corrie to visit more than sixty countries with that redeeming message of hope. Through it all, God taught Corrie something about the power of commitment.

Your faith makes you offer your lives as a sacrifice in serving God. If I have to offer my own blood with your sacrifice, I will be happy and full of joy with all of you.
Philippians 2:17 NCV

wisdom from the past

Most of us are alcoholics when it comes to material things.

Rich Nathan

A Fundamental Shift

The founding document of America references the pursuit of happiness as an "unalienable right" of every individual. Whether or not that can be proved, happiness remains a pursuit that defines most of the human condition. But happiness is a funny thing. Most people pursue it in very tangible terms: possession, comfort, power, and so forth; yet many content people possess few of these commodities, and many people who own them experience a profound discontent. Contentment is a happiness that doesn't fade, but apparently, people are looking in the wrong places.

Could it be that your Designer, your Creator, knows exactly what will bring the deep and abiding satisfaction you crave? The testimony of God's people is that contentment comes, not from amassing natural securities and finite pleasures, but from a supernatural source that is both infinite and expansive. God invites a fundamental shift in thinking: from the external to the internal.

Contentment

the buzz

People who live with circumstance-based satisfaction are doing great when their circumstances are great and doing terrible when circumstances turn sour. Life becomes a roller-coaster ride that whips them from side to side and over gut-churning drops. It's a hard way to live, and one that every person can relate to. But the apostle Paul seemed to have discovered a very different reality: "I have learned to be satisfied with the things I have and with everything that happens" (Philippians 4:11 NCV).

How is that possible? How can satisfaction be so disconnected with the circumstances of your life—from the good things that happen as well as the bad things? That just doesn't seem normal or natural. But what happened was that Paul experienced the shift. Instead of allowing the external forces in his life to shape his internal condition, he released his internal condition upon the external forces in his life.

It's a swing from a circumstance-based satisfaction to an alignment-based satisfaction. Contentment now flows out of Kingdom alignment—a consistent agreement with the values and motivations of heaven that do not swing back and forth as fortunes change. This heavenly alignment is not performance-driven but is identity-driv-

I have learned to be satisfied with the things I have and with everything that happens. I know how to live when I am poor, and I know how to live when I have plenty. I have learned the secret of being happy at any time in everything that happens.
Philippians 4:11–12 NCV

en. In other words, you are content, not because you have done everything right, but because of who you are as a son or daughter of the Kingdom.

This is a happiness that cannot be shaken, as Paul experienced, by either poverty and suffering on the one hand or by abundance and favor on the other. If poverty and abundance are evaluated by external dynamics, then you're missing the point: Your abundance and favor are eternal realities that never cease. It is a greater and enduring reality. And it produced a greater and enduring contentment.

Poverty and suffering are real enough, but they are not the greatest reality. Christians have grappled with these conditions for eons, sometimes through denial, sometimes through an actual glorification of poverty and suffering (the ascetic life). Jesus experienced much poverty and suffering, yet it did not define His internal condition; He constantly experienced the abundance and favor that was His heavenly identity—and so can you.

> When drawn to happiness by good events or to discouragement by bad, dig a little deeper. Burrow down into your truer identity and calling.

When drawn to happiness by good events or to discouragement by bad, dig a little deeper. Burrow down into your truer identity and calling. Get in touch with God's unceasing joy in you, His joy in Himself, and His unwavering joy in a redemptive future. You can afford to be happy and content in God.

Contentment

the insight

It bears mention that God is not anti-happiness. Sometimes pious souls like to talk about "holiness" in lieu of "happiness," but this is an unnecessary and unhelpful division. Holiness—or *alignment*, in the language of this book—is truly the road to happiness, and holy happiness (or happy holiness) is a legitimate, mutually affirming destination for the Christ-follower. Look at what Jesus had to say about happiness in Matthew 5, in what are frequently called the Beatitudes.

> Tempted to political power and sexual sin, Joseph chose integrity. Tempted to discouragement and disillusionment with God, he persevered.

Those people who know they have great spiritual needs are happy, because the kingdom of heaven belongs to them (verse 3 NCV). The world says you're happy when you have no needs, when every desire is satisfied. God says you're happy—or blessed or content—when you understand your spiritual dependency and look for satisfaction in the Kingdom where every spiritual resource belongs to you.

Those who are sad now are happy, because God will comfort them (verse 4 NCV). The world says you're happy when you have no need of comfort. God says you're happy when you know where to look for satisfaction and comfort.

Those who are humble are happy, because the earth will belong to them (verse 5 NCV). The world says happiness comes through power. Ironically,

God promises power to those who do not grasp for it but acknowledge their humble condition.

Those who want to do right more than anything else are happy, because God will fully satisfy them (verse 6 NCV). The world says contentment follows the pursuit of tangible commodities and that these possessions will satisfy. Wrong again! God knows that your internal motivation to pursue righteousness will lead you into contentment and satisfaction because it leads you to Him. And He alone satisfies the human heart more than any possession.

Those who show mercy to others are happy, because God will show mercy to them (verse 7 NCV). The world affirms that those in pursuit of external happiness are an unmerciful lot—they rarely give it and rarely receive it. In contrast, God's children discover that the Kingdom quality of mercy, both given and received, produces an exquisite caliber of happiness in the soul.

Jesus continued through His most famous sermon to call men and women to a joyous life of contentment and showed them where to look. A life of contentment is found, whether in good times or bad, in living true to the Rebellion, true to the Kingdom.

Contentment

the point

Possessions entertain. Possessions soothe. Possessions even facilitate the practical aspects of life. Most aren't wrong or bad. But they cannot satisfy your deeper appetite, and they cannot produce authentic contentment. Happy circumstances tend to bring happy feelings. But contentment runs deeper than circumstances. Lasting happiness is found by those who know their God and who find their place in His redemptive story. Instead of being bounced around by the pinball paddles of outward circumstances, they live out an inner consistency based upon an inner relationship.

the talk

If we have not quiet in our minds, outward comfort will do no more for us than a golden slipper on a gouty foot.

JOHN BUNYAN

The branch of the vine does not worry, and toil, and rush here to seek for sunshine, and there to find rain. No; it rests in union and communion with the vine; and at the right time, and in the right way, is the right fruit found on it. Let us so abide in the Lord Jesus.

HUDSON TAYLOR

God is most glorified in us when we are most satisfied in Him.

JOHN PIPER

Contentment is a pearl of great price, and whoever procures it at the expense of ten thousand desires makes a wise and happy purchase.

JOHN BALGUY

the word

Godliness with contentment is great gain. For we brought nothing into this world, and it is certain we can carry nothing out.

1 Timothy 6:6–7 NKJV

Keep your lives free from the love of money, and be satisfied with what you have. God has said, "I will never leave you; I will never forget you." So we can be sure when we say, "I will not be afraid, because the Lord is my helper. People can't do anything to me."

Hebrews 13:5–6 NCV

Because your love is better than life, I will praise you. I will praise you as long as I live. I will lift up my hands in prayer to your name. I will be content as if I had eaten the best foods. My lips will sing, and my mouth will praise you.

Psalm 63:3–5 NCV

The LORD will always lead you. He will satisfy your needs in dry lands and give strength to your bones. You will be like a garden that has much water, like a spring that never runs dry.

Isaiah 58:11 NCV

There is one alone, without companion: he has neither son nor brother. Yet there is no end to all his labors, nor is his eye satisfied with riches. But he never asks, "For whom do I toil and deprive myself of good?" This also is vanity and a grave misfortune.

Ecclesiastes 4:8 NKJV

Hear, O My people, and I will admonish you! O Israel, if you will listen to Me! . . . Oh, that My people would listen to Me, that Israel would walk in My ways! . . . He would have fed them also with the finest of wheat; and with honey from the rock I would have satisfied you.

Psalm 81:8, 13, 16 NKJV

Contentment

331

the contentment tools

Read it . . .

A Place Called There
Kingsley Fletcher
Where contentment and desire meet.

Cultivating Contentment
Jill Briscoe
Finding contentment by letting go.

Driven No More
Scott Walker
Finding contentment by letting go.

I Long for You, O God
Michael Youssef
Finding rest and contentment in your private worship.

Jesus Is Enough
Claudia May
Experiencing hope, comfort, and contentment in the storms of life.

Keys to Contentment
Sharon Steele
A study of Philippians.

The Rare Jewel of Christian Contentment
J. Burroughs
Achieving true contentment and purpose.

Success God's Way
Charles Stanley
Achieving true contentment and purpose.

Surf it . . .

www.congregationalist.org/Archivesold/Oct-Dec_03/classical_christian_retreats_steece.html
The history and value of classical retreats.

www.godchasers.net
The passionate contentment of Tommy Tenney's ministry.

www.ransomedheart.com
The contented passion of John Eldredge's ministry.

Hear it . . .

A Beautiful Sound, Geoff Moore

Accessed, Delirious?

Barlow Girl, Barlow Girl

Great River Road, Jason Upton

Hear Us Say Jesus, Seven Places

New Direction, New Direction

Pop Culture, Various

Do it . . .

Events with John Piper, www.desiring-god.org/news_events_index.html.

Silent Retreats in the UK, www.leeabbey.org.uk/devon/whatweoffer/silentretreats.php.

The Top Ten Practices of Holy Happiness

10 Allow your inner peace to shape your circumstances, not vice versa.

9 Explore the concept of delighting in the person and ways of God.

8 Hold your desires loosely until confirmed by God's Spirit.

7 Meditate upon the Kingdom abundance and favor that belong to you.

6 Search out the sacrament of the present moment.

5 Learn to ask, "What is God up to in this circumstance?"

4 Differentiate between what is right and what is comfortable.

3 Rest in the security that God works all things for good when you're loving Him.

2 When you're confused or disappointed, trust.

1 Find your greatest satisfaction in fellowship with your Father.

The Question

Have you become

so accustomed to

having your wants

met that you can't

be content having

your needs

fulfilled?

Every person has both needs and wants, and sometimes the line between the two is blurry. Sometimes God lavishes on you what you would call a want but will then later withhold something you're convinced is a need. What gives?

One thing is certain: You "see a dim reflection, as if we were looking into a mirror, but then we shall see clearly. Now I know only a part, but then I will know fully" (1 Corinthians 13:12 NCV). In other words, compared to the brilliant vision of God that guides and directs your life with utter kindness, your perception of what are needs and what are wants is dim.

In a market-driven, advertising-saturated planet, desire can be a compelling force. How do you know if those desires, even good ones, lie within the purpose of God? Simply put, you know by hearing

His voice. When He places divine desire within you that is aligned with Kingdom purpose, you can hold that with confidence. When your desire is met with divine silence or redirection, then the path to contentment lies in releasing that desire as a counterfeit of the real.

Of course, timing is an issue. Even desires that are fully birthed in God's heart for you have to ripen and come into their season. During these times of waiting, there is a divine rub between your vision and your contentment. Maturity is finding a contented peace while trusting God's commitment to His word. What He has promised, He will always deliver. In the meantime, your opportunity is to submit everything you consider either a need or a want to His kind consideration. And then trust His heart toward you.

Sometimes God lavishes on you what you would call a want but will then later withhold something you're convinced is a need. What gives?

There is a freedom for living bound up in this quality of contentment—freedom from striving, freedom from disappointment, freedom to live in the precious gift of now.

Let us then have no other employment, no other ambition but that of uniting our will to the most merciful will of God, and let us be well assured that this will be our salvation even when we imagine that all is lost.
Jean-Pierre de Caussade

Finding Yourself by Losing Yourself

JEAN-PIERRE DE CAUSSADE

1675–1751

Sanctity consists in willing what happens to us by God's order. If we understood how to see in each moment some manifestation of the will of God we should find therein also all that our hearts could desire.

Jean-Pierre de Caussade

"I have known, and do know many saintly people who, for their sole possession have that profound conviction of their weakness, and are never so happy as when they feel themselves, as it were, engulfed in it . . . If you but knew how to walk before Him, your head bowed in this spirit of self-effacement, you would find in it all that makes the spiritual life. It only remains to know how to preserve this spirit of peace and abandonment." So spoke a French Jesuit from the eighteenth century.

There's not a lot known about de Cassaude, born somewhere in the southern French province of Quercy. Reputed to be a quiet and humble man, he was also a mystic and a brilliant spiritual counselor. No images remain of him, and he published only one book anonymously, receding into relative obscurity since then. At the age of eighteen, he became a Jesuit novice and was ordained a priest eleven years later. He taught Greek, Latin, and philosophy in towns near his home in Toulouse, returning to the university for a doctorate in theology. In 1720, Jean-Pierre de Caussade was sent out by his order to preach throughout south-central France.

What is now recognized as his great contribution, the short treatise *Self-Abandonment to Divine Providence,* was pieced together after his death from an array of letters sent to the Nuns of the Visitation, for whom he was a spiritual adviser. This collection grasps the core passion of that God-intoxicated soul: the conviction that every moment of life is a sacrament—a means of grace through which the ordinary and mundane become a channel to experience the magnificence of God and His Kingdom. De Caussade called every disciple to completely abandon himself to the wise direction and mysterious kindness of his heavenly Father. That is contentment.

Whoever desires to save his life will lose it, but whoever loses his life for My sake will find it. For what profit is it to a man if he gains the whole world, and loses his own soul? Or what will a man give in exchange for his soul?
Matthew 16:25–26 NKJV

wisdom from the past

He is the end of our search, not the means to some further end. Our exceeding joy is he, the Lord—not the streets of gold, or the reunion with relatives or any blessing of heaven.

John Piper

The Realm God Rules

Veiled in mystery and wonder, heaven beckons you to peer inside; yet you hesitate. Can anything live up to your hopeful expectation of that place? It plays with your mind because you can't peer inside until you die. Or can you?

Part of the mystery of heaven is that it's not so much a place, in the sense that you normally associate with "place." Heaven is a realm—a sphere of influence that lives and breathes the joyful air of God's rule, a rule so saturated with awe and delight that the human heart cannot contain it, but only wonder and yearn for it.

Fortunately, love is not blind when it comes to heaven. While its fabric eludes mortal inquiry, God has opened up myriad windows that invite closer inspection. Pinpricks of light gleam with a holy radiance and cast a heavenly glow on planet Earth.

Heaven

1 the buzz

eaven has a King, and the domain He rules is called the Kingdom of God or, alternately, the Kingdom of heaven. In heaven, His rule is complete and absolutely transcends earthly imagination. The Bible offers only brief glimpses, but what is seen there confirms that this is your heart's true home—the place you were ultimately made for. It is the epitome of all beauty, all satisfaction, all delight; it is where rest and adventure meet, where truth and mercy kiss; heaven is where the splendor of God fills the vacuous longing of every human heart.

God made a promise to us, and we are waiting for a new heaven and a new earth where goodness lives.
2 Peter 3:13 NCV

Your heart used to be an enemy of that beautiful realm. Perhaps you didn't realize it, but your soul intuitively resisted the lordship of that King in its pursuit of its own will. "My kingdom come, my will be done" is the unspoken decree of the homeless heart until it finds one of those pinpricks into heaven and finds its first glance of Him. Your heart awakens in hope. That saving moment changes you forever, and the rest of your existence becomes the pursuit of that King and that Kingdom.

Your destiny with heaven doesn't begin with death—oh no! It began the day you saw Him and gave up the throne of your heart to that gracious Master. When you did, you became a rebel. Not content to play by the futile, destructive rules of this world's system, you have joined a holy uprising that seeks the rule of God throughout every nook and cranny of His creation. Your goal is nothing less than heaven's rule on earth.

How will that happen? Simply by living true to your new citizenship. The Kingdom life is a supernatural life, one that shines with the transforming energy of God Himself. As your vocation, your marriage, your friendships, and your very soul become aligned with the life of the Kingdom, this world will be infused with heavenly vitality. You don't become perfect, but you do take on a redemptive mission where everything you touch bears a shimmer of heavenly light. All of life becomes a seamless act of worship, and the New Rebellion has come full circle.

Embrace your identity as a child of heaven. Leave behind the hollow excesses of the culture's dictates. Boldly chart a course for Kingdom redemption in your world. Love God and love others with heavenly passion. Then, when you stand on the threshold of heaven itself, your heart will know it has truly come home. Home to the source of all delight!

> Your destiny with heaven doesn't begin with death—oh no! It began the day you saw Him and gave up the throne of your heart to that gracious Master. ✠

341

the insight

Of the few windows Jesus opened into heaven, a great illumination of its values and characteristics is found in the parables of Matthew 13. If you want your life to be aligned with heaven's purpose, align your affections with the things that move God's heart. Let's look at them.

> **T**his world contains a mixture of the heavenly and the worldly. It's not your job to sort them out; that belongs to God. ††

The story of the sower and the seed (verses 3–9): The seed scattered by a farmer is rejected by the hard path, dried up in the rocky soil, and choked out in the thorny patch. It finally finds its home in the tilled, fertile soil. *The window*: There are many distractions to the Kingdom life, including hardness of heart, superficiality, and competing loyalties. But a heaven-centered heart will avoid those diversions and find fruitful purpose.

The story of the wheat and the weeds (verses 24–30): A man sows seed in his field, but an enemy plants weeds among the grain. Instead of removing them immediately, the farmer waits until harvest and then separates the weeds for burning. *The window*: This world contains a mixture of the heavenly and the worldly. It's not your job to sort them out; that belongs to God. Your job is to be the fruitful grain of heaven in this world.

The story of the mustard seed and the yeast (verses 31–33): The tiny mustard seed grows into the largest tree. The smallest ingredient in dough—the yeast—produces the largest, most important result. *The window:* God chose the small, weak things of the world—the people of the New Rebellion—to become the explosive, transforming power of His Kingdom.

The story of the hidden treasure and the pearl (verses 44–46): A man discovers hidden treasure in a field and then sells everything he owns in order to buy that field. Similarly, a merchant searches out the most valuable pearl ever and sells all he possesses to obtain it. *The window*: The New Rebellion isn't something you dabble in recreationally; it is the wholesale investment of your life. A heavenly life requires all and rewards all.

The story of the net (verses 47–50): The fishermen's net hauls up all sorts of fish. But it's not until they get to shore that the good fish are separated from the bad. *The window:* Jesus wants His Kingdom rebels to fight the right fight. It's not about setting everyone straight; it's about living the good news and making that life as attractive as the heaven it represents.

Heaven

the point

The prophet Isaiah promised that God's people "shall be called by a new name" (Isaiah 62:2 NKJV). The apostle John echoed that same promise eight hundred years later: "And I [Jesus] will give him a white stone, and on the stone a new name written which no one knows except him who receives it" (Revelation 2:17 NKJV). This new name is your Kingdom identity: It is who you really are, as seen by heaven's light. It is your heavenly gift to the world.

the talk

If you read history you will find out that the Christians who did most for the present world were precisely those who thought most of the next.

C. S. LEWIS

Earth has no sorrow that Heaven cannot heal.

THOMAS MOORE

The true object of all human life is play. Earth is a task garden; heaven is a playground.

G. K. CHESTERTON

The really good news for Christians is that Jesus is now taking students in the master class of life. So the message of and about him is specifically a gospel for our life now, not just for dying. It is about living now as his apprentices in kingdom living, not just as consumers of his merits.

DALLAS WILLARD

the word

From that time Jesus began to preach and to say, "Repent, for the kingdom of heaven is at hand."

Matthew 4:17 NKJV

Jesus told them another story: "The kingdom of heaven is like a man who planted good seed in his field. That night, when everyone was asleep, his enemy came and planted weeds among the wheat and then left."

Matthew 13:24–25 NCV

God's kingdom is like a treasure hidden in a field for years and then accidentally found by a trespasser . . . Or, God's kingdom is like a jewel merchant on the hunt for excellent pearls.

Matthew 13:44–45 MSG

The kingdom of heaven is like a net that was put into the lake and caught many different kinds of fish. When it was full, the fishermen pulled the net to the shore. They sat down and put all the good fish in baskets and threw away the bad fish.

Matthew 13:47–48 NCV

Jesus answered, "You have been chosen to know the secrets about the kingdom of heaven . . . That seed [on the rocks] is like the person who hears the message about the kingdom but does not understand it . . . [The good] seed is like the person who hears the teaching and understands it."

Matthew 13:11, 19, 23 NCV

Jesus told another story: "The kingdom of heaven is like a mustard seed that a man planted in his field . . ." Then Jesus told another story: "The kingdom of heaven is like yeast that a woman took and hid in a large tub of flour until it made all the dough rise."

Matthew 13:31, 33 NCV

Heaven

the heaven tools

Read it . . .

EKG
Ken Hemphill
Empowering Kingdom growth—the heartbeat of God.

Heaven
Randy Alcorn
Comprehensive biblical answers to your questions.

Heaven: My Father's House
Anne Graham Lotz
Heaven as home, refuge, and God's ultimate vision.

The Insider
Jim Petersen and Mike Shamy
Bringing the Kingdom of God into your everyday world.

Laughter from Heaven
Barbara Johnson
Humorous views on our heavenly home.

Let the Nations Be Glad!
John Piper
The supremacy of God in missions.

The Slumber of Christianity
Ted Dekker
Awakening a passion for heaven on earth.

Triumphant Return
Grant R. Jeffrey
The coming Kingdom of God.

Surf it . . .

www.christiananswers.net
Forty thousand answers to tough questions, plus movie reviews and cultural critique.

www.fillthevoid.org/Christian/Heaven.html
Biblical descriptions of your heavenly home.

archives.cnn.com/2001/COMMUNITY/12/11/graham.lotz/index.html
CNN's interview with Anne Graham Lotz on heaven and 9/11.

Hear it . . .

Day of Fire, Day of Fire

Disappear, PFR

Free to Fly, Vineyard

Kingdom Come, Charlie Peacock

Only Visiting This Planet, Larry Norman

Over Blue City, Skypark

Spoken For, Mercy Me

Trading My Sorrows: The Best of Darrell Evans, Darrell Evans

Do it . . .

Conferences, resources, and passion for the Bridegroom, www.fotb.com.

Make a heavenly difference in the world with YWAM, www.ywam.org.

TOP TEN

The Top Ten Evidences of Heaven's Aroma on Earth

10 Hope in the midst of cynicism.

9 Contentment in the midst of adverse circumstances.

8 Genuine care for others in a self-centered world.

7 Willing sacrifice of all the world holds dear for unseen reward.

6 Unified community in an angry, fractured culture.

5 Courage to gamble all of life upon a spiritual vision.

4 A tenacious joy that is unexplainable in worldly terms.

3 Supernatural healing of body, mind, and spirit.

2 Love for enemies.

1 Forgiveness.

I must keep alive in myself the desire for my true country, which I shall not find till after death; I must never let it get snowed under or turned aside; I must make it the main object of life to press on to that other country and to help others to do the same.

C. S. Lewis

The Question

Does your belief

in heaven change

the way you live

on earth?

There can be nothing more tragic than a life re-created by the light of heaven that hides its true identity and remains cloaked in the darkness of this world's system. The loss to the Kingdom is simply off the charts. Jesus alluded to this in Matthew 5:14–16: "You are the light that gives light to the world. A city that is built on a hill cannot be hidden. And people don't hide a light under a bowl. They put it on a lampstand so the light shines for all the people in the house. In the same way, you should be a light for other people" (NCV).

This call to shine in the world was never intended to be an "ought" of obligation but rather a glorious privilege. And so it is. It isn't putting on a religious show. It isn't being weird or strange. It is simply being true to who you now are. It's living honestly in a dishonest world.

A life infused with heaven's radiance is a life that's not filtered in order to fit in. You're not putting anything on, and you're not filtering anything out. You are allowing God to send out an enticing aroma from your life, like the aroma from a pizza parlor. Paul described the dynamic this way: "We are to God the fragrance of Christ among those who are being saved and among those who are perishing. To the one we are the aroma of death leading to death, and to the other the aroma of life leading to life" (2 Corinthians 2:15–16 NKJV).

A life infused with heaven's radiance is a life that's not filtered in order to fit in.

You can expect your heavenly aroma to have a polarizing effect on people—they will be either attracted or repulsed, according to their heart condition. And this is God's intention in the world: to set the table and invite all, allowing men and women the freedom to choose or not choose life.

If your heart takes more pleasure in reading novels, or watching TV, or going to the movies, or talking to friends, rather than just sitting alone with God and embracing Him, sharing His cares and His burdens, weeping and rejoicing with Him, then how are you going to handle forever and ever in His presence?
Keith Green

Building the Kingdom

KINGSLEY FLETCHER
Church Planter

We are living in crucial times! This is not a time for popularity contests. It is a time for action. We want to be known as a servant ministry which is obedient to the mandate of taking his life and peace to the world while preparing people for his Kingdom!

Kingsley Fletcher

Dr. Kingsley Fletcher has a unique perspective on the Kingdom of heaven, and that's because he is a king himself. He left Ghana, West Africa, in the late seventies to dedicate his life to spreading the message of Jesus to the world. His travels have taken him to more than a hundred countries, where he has planted more than two hundred churches and become fluent in thirteen languages. In 1999, Fletcher was crowned as Drolor Bosso Adamtey I, Shai King for Progress and Development, fulfilling his birthright and strengthening his commitment to help bring the African continent into the twenty-first century.

Residing in North America for more than twenty years, Dr. Fletcher has continued his mandate of teaching the truth to every nation and every tribe. He believes he was born for such a time as this—to see people around the world set free through the power of God. Today God is speaking to the darkest nations of the world and empowering the disenfranchised with His love.

Fletcher is convinced that those who have been bound into a life of physical slavery will now be used of God to bring spiritual freedom to the world. Soon missionaries from the continents of Africa, Asia, and South America will go into North America and Europe to teach about the grace, love, and power of the living God. Part of Fletcher's calling is to teach and equip these believers to be a blessing to all nations.

The vision of Kingsley Fletcher Ministries is to set people free through the power of God's Spirit and equip believers for the end-time harvest, while building genuine unity in the body of Christ. Their mission is to bring God's love, healing, restoration, and power to the people of all nations. And they're doing it. Fletcher is truly an earthly king building a heavenly Kingdom.

Let not your heart be troubled; you believe in God, believe also in Me. In My Father's house are many mansions; if it were not so, I would have told you. I go to prepare a place for you. And if I go and prepare a place for you, I will come again and receive you to Myself; that where I am, there you may be also.
John 14:1–3 NKJV

wisdom from the now

Tears shed for self are tears of weakness, but tears shed for others are a sign of strength.

Billy Graham

I beg you to offer your lives as a living sacrifice to him. Your offering must be only for God and pleasing to him, which is the spiritual way for you to worship. Do not change yourselves to be like the people of this world, but be changed within by a new way of thinking.

Romans 12:1–2 NCV

Why, then, do we worry about recession, cartels, changes in world leadership, and ungodliness? Can they stop God from presenting to this world a Church which is glorious, spotless, and full of the power of God?

Judson Cornwall

Are you tired? Worn out?
Burned out on religion?
Come to me. Get away with
me and you'll recover your
life…Walk with me and
work with me—watch how
I do it. Learn the unforced
rhythms of grace…Keep
company with me and
you'll learn to live freely
and lightly.

Matthew 11:28–30 MSG

When we know love matters more than anything, and we know that nothing else really matters, we move into the state of surrender. Surrender does not diminish our power; it enhances it.

Sara Paddison

We are prepared to serve the Lord only by sacrifice. We are fit for the work of God only when we have wept over it, prayed about it, and then we are enabled by Him to tackle the job that needs to be done. May God give to us hearts that bleed, eyes that are wide open to see, minds that are clear to interpret God's purposes, wills that are obedient, and a determination that is utterly unflinching as we set about the tasks He would have us to do.

Alan Redpath

He is no fool who gives what he cannot keep to gain what he cannot lose.

Jim Elliot

Whoever wants to be great must become a servant. Whoever wants to be first among you must be your slave. That is what the Son of Man has done: He came to serve, not be served— and then to give away his life in exchange for the many who are held hostages.

Matthew 20:27–28 MSG

God chose you to be his people,
so I urge you now to live the
life to which God called you.

Ephesians 4:1 NCV